Jonathan Edwards: *Theologian*
of
the Heart

Jonathan Edwards: *Theologian of the Heart*

by Harold
P. Simonson

WILLIAM B. EERDMANS PUBLISHING COMPANY
Grand Rapids/Michigan

Library of Congress Cataloging in Publication Data

Simonson, Harold Peter, 1926-
  Jonathan Edwards: theologian of the heart.

  Includes bibliographical references.
  1. Edwards, Jonathan, 1703-1758. I. Title.
BX7260.E3S56   285'.8'0924 [B]   74-4494
ISBN 0-8028-3448-5

For my family
especially remembering St. Andrews

Contents

Preface

For the primary sources of this study I have depended mainly upon the 1834 edition of *The Works of Jonathan Edwards* (2 vols.), edited by Edward Hickman and containing the valuable Memoir by Edwards' grandson, Sereno E. Dwight. Except where specifically noted, documentation of Edwards' writing refers to this edition. To facilitate the citing of references, I have incorporated most of them, as indicated, into the written text. It must be noted, however, that when referring to works of Edwards now available in the new Yale editions, I have chosen these editions rather than that of Hickman. The Yale volumes include *Freedom of the Will* (ed. Paul Ramsey), *A Treatise Concerning Religious Affections* (ed. John E. Smith), *Original Sin* (ed. Clyde E. Holbrook), and *The Great Awakening* (ed. C. C. Goen). In this latter volume, whose title is supplied by Professor Goen, are found Edwards' *A Faithful Narrative, The Distinguishing Marks,* and *Some Thoughts Concerning the Revival.* When referring to each of these three works, I cite the Goen edition. I also use the single works edited by Perry Miller and William K. Frankena when I treat Edwards' *Images and Shadows of Divine Things* and *The Nature of True Virtue* respectively.

The major portion of this book was written in St. Andrews, Scotland. The faculty of St. Mary's College and the staff of the University library extended many courtesies that I will long remember. It is a particular pleasure to acknowledge the helpful suggestions of Professor J. K. Cameron, who read an early draft of the manuscript, and the conversations with Professor N. H. G. Robinson, Professor James Whyte, and Principal Matthew Black. I would be remiss if I failed to mention the kindness of James and Maud Harrison, and Arthur and Emmine McAllister, with whom I will

9

always associate Scottish generosity at its best. I owe the greatest gratitude to my wife Carolyn and my three children—Eric, Greta, and Peter—whose affections supported me as I studied those of Edwards.

—H. P. S.
University of Washington

Introduction

In his book *Fear and Trembling* Søren Kierkegaard recounts the Abraham-Isaac story, literally telling it again and again, and each time seeing in it added richness, complexity, and power. His retelling the story is meant to suggest the way he himself returned to it after having first read it as a boy. Something about the story compelled him to do so, and during subsequent years his oft-repeated reading increased his certainty that here was an enigma, the enigma of religious faith, that demanded his total attention. Abraham's faith irresistibly drew Kierkegaard to ever deeper levels of understanding, and it was from these depths that he wrote his book.

Although a century and an ocean separated the two thinkers, something of this same profound urgency possessed the mind of Jonathan Edwards. He too had been awakened early in his life to the mystery of religion, and had been similarly struck by the haunting power of Biblical words. In his case they were those of St. Paul: "Now unto the King eternal, immortal, invisible, the only wise God, be honour and glory for ever and ever" (I Timothy 1:17). "Never any words of Scripture seemed to me as these words did," he wrote in his *Personal Narrative*. There came into his soul, he said, "a sense of the glory of the Divine Being; a new sense, quite different from any thing I ever experienced before." Through the years he orchestrated these words into a magnificent corpus of writing which sustained the theme of God's glory and the sense of it in the human heart. Edwards experienced this effulgence to a greater extent than Kierkegaard did; nevertheless, there was in both writers a religious passion that dominated their lives and a sense of the heart that infused their words, to the extent that today's reader finds himself strangely compelled to return again and again to their writing.

In this present study I have analyzed Edwards' sense of the heart. I have chosen to do so because, in the first place, this approach has not played a dominant part in the scholarship on Edwards. Perry Miller, the foremost modern interpreter of Edwards, stresses a Lockean epistemology, and in doing so fails to give sufficient note to the heart-felt pietism that was the foundation of Edwards' life and thought. The second reason for drawing attention to what can be called an epistemology of religious conversion is that it informs Edwards' whole theology. Edwards himself never allowed empirical science to define the nature of religious experience; William James did so a century and a half later, and Miller bases his interpretation of Edwards upon similar propositions. Whatever seventeenth- and eighteenth-century intellectual influences worked upon Edwards, the essential ones go back to John Calvin, back further to St. Augustine, and finally to St. Paul. The point has to do with religious conversion, with the unreasonable, offensive, and radical fact of divine grace. From this, according to Edwards, all subsequent knowledge springs. Or, to state the matter differently, whatever is not of the redeemed heart is finally to be regarded as no real knowledge at all. In holding to this position Edwards now can be seen standing alongside Kierkegaard who, in *The Sickness Unto Death,* reiterated the Pauline doctrine that whatever is not of faith is sin. In epistemological terms, what we know depends upon what we are. Edwards spent a lifetime declaring that what we are depends upon the heart, the redeemed and sanctified heart.

In order to prepare the groundwork for Edwards' theory of the heart, I devote the two initial chapters to the fact of religious experience as it first relates to Edwards' biography and then to his New England times. His early years as a student at Yale and then as a fledgling minister at Northampton, Massachusetts; his reading of John Locke; his theological concerns that steadily showed the influence of Calvin as well as Locke—all are seen as important matters preceding his clarion statements of 1731 and 1734 on the sovereignty of God and justification by faith, respectively. These important pronouncements establishing his Calvinist position initiated theological disputes that shaped his entire career. These doctrines, representative of his sweeping opposition to Arminian liberalism, were also the basis for the religious revivalism that by 1735 had spread through the Connecticut Valley.

It was not Edwards' intrepid defense of Calvinism *per se* that made his leadership during the Awakening most notable; it was rather his profound conviction that Calvinist theology was experientially true. He was convinced that human experience corroborates Calvin's insights. Edwards insisted that unless theology was rooted in experience, it could not be anything more than intellectual speculation. In going beyond Locke's theory of sensation, Edwards vitalized the doctrines of original sin, justification by grace, election, and salvation, and provided the spiritual tone for the whole Awakening.

To make revivalism theologically convincing, Edwards had to distinguish between emotionalism and true religious affections. Revivalist ministers were being attacked (sometimes justifiably) for failing to appreciate the distinction, and Edwards himself cautioned them as to its importance. Most notable among his early writings on the subject were *Distinguishing Marks of a Work of the Spirit of God* (1741) and *Some Thoughts Concerning the Present Revival of Religion in New England* (1743), works that contemporary readers regardless of their theological leanings recognized as remarkable treatises in their own right. When *A Treatise Concerning Religious Affections* appeared in 1746, there was no mistaking that a major voice was among them. Even though this work appeared after the Great Awakening had run its course, it clarified once and for all its author's basic stance. Religion, he asserted, consists not merely in speculative understanding but in will, inclination, affection. Religion is a matter of true affections that incline the heart away from self-love and towards God. What this means in terms of experience was Edwards' life-long theme.

In the next two chapters (3 and 4) I discuss what in Edwards' theology are important consequences of religious experience. Specifically, I concern myself with imagination (vision) and language. These more speculative chapters of the book take up what Edwards only occasionally made explicit but what nevertheless undergirded his great preaching on sin and salvation. Edwards believed that knowing depends upon the knower, and that all Christian knowledge bears upon the experience of conversion. This meant that imagination as an endowment of natural man embraces nothing spiritual unless the soul (the heart) through faith first embraces God. In short, man first believes so that he can truly imagine, perceive, see. According to Edwards, sanctified imagination enables one to grasp what to natural man is invisible and unknowable. One thereby sees everything as images or shadows of divine things and as existing within the unity of divine meaning. When envisioned from within the circle of Christian faith, everything is divine emanation. Only within this context, which Edwards identified as Christian revelation, can human imagination be trusted. Only when the soul "closes" with Christ and grace illumines the heart does the aesthetic vision become Christian, and the artist become saint.

Religious language is faith-language. In coming to this view, Edwards sharply veered away from Locke, who conceived of words as arbitrary signs imposed upon ideas and having no inseparable connection with them. To Locke, words come after ideas and bear only arbitrary relation to them. Edwards, on the other hand, connected words to actual ideas (an *actual* idea was always, in Edwards' view, an event, always an experience involving emotion as well as ratiocination), so that words serve to bridge knowledge and being, cognition and apprehension. He went even further by attempting to connect words to religious experience. Of course he failed in this, as he realized he must. He knew the limitations of religious language, though they were not as restrictive as those of aesthetics. Religious language, Edwards said, can never fully express the sense of the heart. Neither can it be the final means of grace. Words are the "occasional" cause, never the "sufficient" cause; they prepare the heart by creating an emotional readiness for the apprehension of religious truth, but they are never the sufficient means of conveying it.

As preacher and writer, Edwards used words as a means to prepare the heart of listener and reader. In the last two chapters (5 and 6) I explore ways Edwards did this, especially as he gave expression to the great Christian doctrines of sin and salvation. Regarding his treatment of sin, I give special attention to "Sinners in the Hands of an Angry God," the most famous sermon ever preached by anyone in America. On the subject of salvation, I discuss Edwards' ideas pertaining both to personal salvation and to salvation-history, including his ideas of creation and eschatology. In both chapters the main attention is upon his sermons, though commentary upon them necessarily requires examination of the underlying theology established by Edwards in certain non-homiletic works. Of particular importance in this connection are such works as *Original Sin* (1758),

The Nature of True Virtue (1765), and *Concerning the End for Which God Created the World* (1765).

The emphasis throughout the book is upon what Edwards called the sense of the heart—the capacity beyond Lockean sensationalism, beyond ratiocination, beyond speculation and "understanding," beyond aesthetic vision—the capacity, through faith, finally to experience God's glory and to see it as the ultimate end and purpose of His creation.

CHAPTER ONE

Edwards' Record of Conversion

1
The Awakened Heart

What we know of Jonathan Edwards' early life, particularly of his religious emotions—before he was ordained at Northampton in 1727 at the age of twenty-three—comes chiefly from three short writings that he never intended the public to read. One is his *Personal Narrative*, written sometime after 1739, probably when Edwards was about forty years old. This work is commonly and justifiably recognized as one of the great autobiographies in American literature. Fully two-thirds of it concerns these early years of Edwards' life, viewed from a perspective benefited by many more years of mature reflection. The second document is a *Diary* that Edwards started on December 18, 1722, when he was nineteen, and finished some four years later, although, to be accurate, one should note that Edwards added a single short entry in 1728, another in 1734, and three in 1735. The third work is what Edwards called *Resolutions*, numbering seventy, all written before he was twenty. Taken together, these three pieces span the six years Edwards was an undergraduate and a graduate student of theology at Yale (up to 1722); the eight months he served as minister in a Scottish Presbyterian church in New York (from August 1722 to April 1723); and the period prior to his election as tutor at Yale, the two years in that post, and the few months prior to his ordination at Northampton on February 15, 1727—the occasion, said his grandson and biographer Sereno Dwight, of Edwards' "entering on the business of life."[1]

In considering Edwards' theology of the heart and its basis in the redemptive experience of religion, it is necessary to look at these early years for what they reveal about his own religious life. One thing is certain from these three documents: from an early age Edwards was persistently concerned with the mysterious world of religion. In the first place, his family and surroundings nurtured this interest. His father, Timothy Edwards, was the minister for sixty-four years at East Windsor, Jonathan's birthplace, remaining in the pulpit until his death at the age of eighty-nine in 1758, just two months before his son's death. Furthermore, Jonathan's maternal grandfather was the venerable Solomon Stoddard, for decades the most influential minister in the Connecticut Valley. Jonathan's maternal grandmother, Esther Warham Mather, was the daughter of John Warham, first minister to the Connecticut Colony, and the granddaughter of Thomas Hooker, the mightiest of all first-generation Puritan preachers in America. Lineage, however, never satisfactorily explains genius, nor does it fully account for a child's predilections, such as Edwards' practice when only a boy of seven or eight to retire to a secret "booth" he built in the swampy woods outside East Windsor and there, with certain schoolmates, to pray and "spend much time in religious conversation." He wrote in his *Personal Narrative* that even at that early age, before he entered the Connecticut "Collegiate School" (Yale's original name) at thirteen, his affections "seemed to be lively and easily moved," and that he seemed in his element when engaged in "religious duties" (I,liv).

To follow these years prior to the time Edwards began his monumental work at Northampton starts one, as it were, along a pilgrimage of grace that, like so many features of Edwards' life, began remarkably early. The record seems written in the agony as well as the jubilation of God's felt presence. An intensity permeates the record, as if from an early age Edwards knew that the truly fundamental business of life concerned religion. Solid as this conviction was, he also realized that such a pilgrimage includes profound experiences of dread and even terror. Thus we repeatedly find that Edwards' resolutions to seek salvation and to do what befits God's glory were offset by melancholy, rebellion, and despair. Even when he seemed "fully satisfied" as to the doctrines of God's sovereignty, judgment, and election, he grew uneasy when his mind "rested" in these doctrines. That the words in I Timothy 1:17—"Now unto the King eternal, immortal, invisible, the only wise God, be honour and glory for ever and ever"—brought to him a new sense of God's glory, a sense radically different from anything ever experienced before, also left him restless to understand the saving nature of the experience and sometimes stricken by its terrifying power. *Personal Narrative* portrays young Edwards as totally engaged within the dynamics of faith, necessarily including both peace and despair. But were we to suspect that Edwards, writing this document in his middle years, was consciously creating a mere *persona* that represented in dramatic terms the universality of his experience, a simple collation with both the *Diary* and *Resolutions* indicates that he was in fact honestly recalling his adolescence as a time of titanic inner turmoil, terribly private and subjective.

A notable confluence of these three documents concerns the date January 12, 1723, as closely as one can pinpoint the occasion of Edwards' religious conversion. At this time Edwards was nineteen years old; he had completed six years at Yale and was now half through his short ministry in New York. Some twenty years later in his *Personal Narrative* he wrote of this day: "I made a solemn dedication of myself to God, and wrote it down; giving up myself, and all that I had, to God; to be for the future in no respect my own; to act as one that had no right to himself, in any respect" (I,lvi). In his *Resolutions* for the same day he wrote: *"Resolved,* That no other end but religion shall have any influence at all on any of my actions; and that no action shall be, in the least circumstance, any otherwise than the religious end will carry it" (I,lxii). And in his *Diary* for this same Saturday appears an entry of over 900 words, by far the longest single entry in the entire document. Written at different times during the day, the statement records his experience of the morning: "I have been before God, and have given myself, all that I am and have, to God" (I,lxvii). In the afternoon he teased the question whether after his commitment he should allow himself the "delight or satisfaction" of friends, food, and "animal [natural] spirits." His affirmative answer carried the qualification that such joy should "help religion."

Of equal concern was the extent to which he felt he must devote himself to religious activities, even at the cost of his health. He had reason enough to worry, for he never enjoyed physical robustness commensurate with a spiritual kind. According to Dwight, he was "tender and feeble" even at the typically hale age of twenty-three, and he preserved his tolerable health only with "unceasing care" (I,lxxviii). It is noteworthy that extended illness interrupted his tutorial teaching at Yale, and other illness delayed by several months his assuming the full duties at Northampton after Stoddard's death in February 1729 had vacated the pulpit to the young successor. Therefore, the concern that Edwards manifested on this important day in 1723 is understandable. Yet with unrelenting severity he questioned whether his desire for occasional ease eventuated from a kind of deceptive weariness that hid sloth rather than from genuine tiredness. Whatever might be its origin, he vowed that physical weariness would not deter him from his work—from prayers, study, writing, and memorizing sermons. His notation in the evening makes this clear: "It is no matter how much tired and weary I am" (I,lxvii). Clearly, Edwards conceived his religious commitment as demanding the whole self—body, mind, and spirit.

But as John Bunyan's pilgrim knew, even at the very gates of glory there leads a byway to the pit. The pit opened almost immediately for Edwards. Only three days later he lamented: "It seemed yesterday, the day before, and Saturday, that I should always retain the same resolutions to the same height. But alas! how soon do I decay! O how weak, how infirm, how unable to do any thing of myself! What a poor inconsistent being! What a miserable wretch, without the assistance of the Spirit of God!" (I,lxviii). Two days later on January 17 he wrote that he was "overwhelmed with melancholy" (I,lxviii). This struggle for faith does not necessarily imply that Edwards doubted the ground of faith itself. Nor should we think that Edwards' torment came from unbelief. Simply put, his doubts arose from what he considered his uncertain relationship with God. Now for the first time the feeling of true dependency stirred within, painfully informing him that in spite of all his resolutions he was still a creature dependent upon God's assistance. What he further recognized was his own inconsistency, the shocking truth that the good he would resolve to do he was not able to do. Here was St. Paul's insight, and here too was Paul's lament in Romans 7: "O wretched man that I am!" As the apostle knew, the problem was not one of will. "To will," he said, "is present with me; but *how* to perform that which is good I find not" (7:18). Whatever it cost Paul in inward travail to write Romans 8, he affirmed that the "how" depended upon divine grace effected within a relationship of man's dependency upon God. So deeply was this truth seared upon Edwards' heart that eight years later, in 1731, when honored to preach before Boston's clerical elite, he chose the same theme, "God

Glorified in Man's Dependence," a sermon that made his position unequivocally clear to the agitated Arminians sitting in the congregation.

It was during these final months in New York that Edwards experienced not only the first fruits of the Spirit but their concomitant cost. In Pauline terms his whole being did groan in pain. During the next three years his *Diary* records few instances of relief, even though, as hopeful counterpoint, he drafted still more resolutions. Especially while he was a tutor at Yale, the record shows a deeply brooding and melancholic mind. Partial explanation stems from the troubles that still rocked the College from the 1722 insurrection when Rector Timothy Cutler, a tutor, and two neighboring ministers renounced Congregationalism and, in loyalty to the legal government, declared themselves Episcopalians. When Edwards took up his duties in May 1724 the College was still without a Head. Except for the trustees who alternately served as vice-rector, only three tutors, including Edwards, constituted the active staff. It was, then, upon them that the daily administrative and instructional tasks fell. Caught in this tangle only a month, Edwards could already speak of "despondencies, fears, perplexities, multitudes of cares, and distraction of mind" (I,lxxvii). And three months later: "Crosses of the nature of that which I met with this week, thrust me quite below all comforts in religion" (I,lxxvii). By the following June he wrote of being so "listless" that nothing but conversation or bodily exercise offered respite. His single entry for 1726 summarized the whole difficult period: " 'Tis just about three years, that I have been for the most part in a low sunk estate and condition, miserably senseless, to what I used to be, about spiritual things" (I,lxxviii).

Evident from these years is the fact that Edwards' conversion was not an instantaneous happening but rather a succession of deepening disturbances that relentlessly quickened in him both the sense of his natural weakness, even wretchedness, and the sense of divine grace. Rarely did he know calmness or what he later called "sweet complacency in God" without also being conscious of disturbing tremors deep within. His *Personal Narrative* becomes most compelling when he describes not only his desire to be swallowed up in Christ but also his pervasive sense of unworthiness. Neither his arrival in Northampton in 1727 to share the pulpit with his illustrious grandfather nor his marriage the same year to Sarah Pierrepont dissolved these antipodal feelings. Instead, his growing consciousness of the "sweet and glorious" doctrines of the gospel only measured, by contrast, the sense of his "infinite wickedness." The significance of this twofold sense derived from the nature of religious maturity. The point, of course, is not that Edwards had grown more wicked but that his deepened consciousness enabled him to see himself more transparently. As with Paul, who though regenerated yet saw himself as "the chief of sinners," so also with Edwards, who though blessed by God's "sweet grace and love" nonetheless thought himself as one deserving "the lowest place in hell." In both instances conversion meant a new understanding of oneself in relation to God.

Although it is important to recognize Edwards' youth as a time of fervent religious awakening, it is even more crucial to remember that Edwards' religious experiences, whether involving a sense of sin or of holiness, constituted the foundation of his life. To miss this fact is to miss the essential meaning of all that he later wrote. Few persons in American intellectual history rooted their written word more profoundly in private experience. For Edwards this experience was a Christian one. Doctrines of sin and salvation, of judgment, grace, and election, were ingredients of this reality. They were defended by him because he experienced this reality, not because he wished to defend Calvinism *per se.* What Edwards repeatedly called "a sense of the heart" originated from this personal, experiential sense.

It can, of course, be argued that the force behind Edwards' major treatises was also polemical, and that these works were directed towards specific men and theological issues of the day. Thus, for example, his *Treatise Concerning Religious Affections* answered the rationalists; his *Humble Inquiry* concerning the qualifications for communion answered those persons even within his own congregation who supported Stoddardeanism and the Half-Way Covenant; his *Freedom of the Will* clearly took all Arminians for its target; and his *Doctrine of Original Sin* served as a direct reply to the Rev. John Taylor.

Yet the point deserves reiteration that Edwards intended his great intellectual treatises to find their corroboration in the human heart. His own religious affections impelled their composition. A distinguishing feature implicit in his whole theology, even when most coldly polemical, is the centrality he gives to man and his condition of the heart—always in relation to God. If, as John Macquarrie suggests, an existential theology presupposes man as a unique "I" distinct from nature and personally responsible before God, then Edwards can be called existential.[2] Edwards saw himself in this relational light and believed that only as man first is separated from nature can he know true being and uniqueness. Thus his destiny is realized not as he loses himself in nature, not as he retains his fallenness within it, but only as he receives grace to live apart from nature and in relationship with a personal God of history—a wrathful, gracious, living God. Such a God is never merely the Unmoved Mover, the First Cause, the Timeless Absolute. Neither is he the God of philosophical speculation and understanding. Echoing Pascal, Edwards declared that God is the God of Abraham, Isaac, Jacob—indeed the sovereign God of Northampton's own outsetting minister and theologian.

2
Locke and Empiricism

The two basic factors in Edwards' psychology were (1) the speculative or notional and (2) the intuitive. The former he also termed "understanding," the latter he called "will," "inclination," "affection"—or "the sense of the heart." In the present study we are chiefly concerned with the latter, and we have already noticed how Edwards' early *Diary* and *Resolutions,* as well as his autobiographical masterpiece, *Personal Narrative,* take their whole coloration from this affectional side of his experience. Considering that these writings so intimately treat his experiences during the years at Yale, it may not be surprising to discover that in these three pieces he alludes to no other books than Scripture. This fact suggests the primacy as well as privacy with which he regarded his deepening religious convictions.

We know, however, that the curriculum at Yale included Latin, Greek, Hebrew, Ramist rhetoric, and logic, and that among its standard fare were William Ames's *Medulla* and *Theological Theses and Cases.* From the essay on rainbows Edwards wrote before entering Yale it appears he had read Sir Isaac Newton's *Opticks,* and as a college student he devoured John Locke's *An Essay Concerning*

Human Understanding. In his senior year he specifically asked his father to send him "Alstead's Geometry and Gassendus' Astronomy" plus *The Art of Thinking* by Antoine Arnauld and Pierre Nicolet.[3] The more we examine these formative years, the more evident it is that matching Edwards' growing religious consciousness was an equally impressive intellectual development. Granted that the two sides cannot be arbitrarily separated. Yet Edwards insisted upon a twofold nature of knowledge, and during his student years he formulated what superficially resembled this division of categories. The even more important point suggests that Edwards at this time was trying to understand the whole phenomenon of mind itself, a phenomenon that he was verifying daily in his own emotional and intellectual life. It is instructive to observe the way Edwards pursued his task.

When he was sixteen and a Yale senior, he wrote what has been called "one of the most tantalizing documents in American intellectual history."[4] Bearing the name *Notes on "The Mind,"* the work consists of seventy-two entries, some only a few sentences long, others substantial paragraphs. Within the *Notes* are two entries worthy to be called essays—"Of Being" and "The Prejudices of Imagination"—and at the end of the *Notes* an outline that he apparently intended to use for a projected but unwritten Treatise on the Mind. Admirably reconstructed by Professor Leon Howard, this entire document reveals the intellectual awakening of the Edwards who would become America's greatest eighteenth-century mind. One could go further back in Edwards' "intellectual" writing to those remarkable little pieces done before he entered Yale—essays on the soul, flying spiders, and rainbows. But it is with the *Notes* that we have the first solid indication that here was a young man of astonishing intellectual acuity.

That John Locke was a major force behind this growth does not for a moment lessen the claim that Edwards, even as a youth, was an independent thinker. To the college student Locke's *Essay* was indeed a treasure—like "handfuls of silver and gold," said Samuel Hopkins, Edwards' personal friend and earliest biographer[5]—containing serene speculations about the mind and its perception of reality. Although seized by Locke's ideas, Edwards remained restive, always wishing to push beyond Locke and wanting more than Locke gave.

Young Edwards found Locke's concept of natural cause and effect attractive because it implied universal design, but he also speculated further about the nature of the design. He attributed to it teleological qualities of equality, correspondency, symmetry, and regularity. He thought of it in terms of harmony and proportion. He ventured still further to the Idealist's position of seeing all matter and proportions as "shadows" of supreme being in unitary proportion.

Whether or not at this point he read George Berkeley is of less importance than the fact that Edwards' own remarkably careful thought led him to an early Idealism.[6] Implied in it was a Creator or Divine Mind in whom all things coalesce in perfect harmony. The essence of this harmony is divine love. Edwards' analogy is specific: "When one thing sweetly harmonizes with another, as the notes in musick, the notes are so conformed, and have such proportion one to another, that they seem to have respect one to another, as if they loved one another. So the beauty of figures and motions is . . . very much the image of Love." The "sweet harmony" among the many parts of the universe becomes the image of "mutual love." What Locke had conceived as natural law signified to Edwards a universe in which all things consent to the whole in love. In such consent was to be found true Being or, in one of Edwards' great terms, true "excellency." Edwards here was wrestling with a concept by which he hoped to reconcile finite and infinite being. Such reconciliation occurs, he thought, when the one consents to the other. In short, excellency is that apotheosis when being consents to Being. The nature of this consent is love: "Spiritual Excellency is resolved into Love."[7]

These are majestic ideas for one at any age, but Edwards at sixteen had only just begun. He had established the Creator as infinite Being and as the perfection of excellency. He had argued that all matter, including man's natural world, subsists within and through infinite Being. And he had shown that true excellency consists in the act of consenting in love. These are ideas he would refine to brilliance in later writing.

The *Notes* show that many other intellectual problems engaged the youthful Edwards at New Haven. He seemed ready to settle upon the Lockean concept of sensation as the source of what the mind knows. To Locke all knowledge depended upon ideas shaped by sense experience. Yet Edwards wondered about the real source of these sensations that are transmitted to the mind. Do sensations "carry the appearance" of a supreme, willing Being? Furthermore, is the mind as passive in receiving them as Locke had said it was? To Edwards the mind seemed "abundantly active." Memory, imagination, judgment were all faculties of the mind subsisting in activity. Edwards claimed, for example, that even in idle moments the imagination arranges "marks or spots in the floor or wall" into "regular parcels and figures."[8] Obviously not all the questions he was raising about the nature of sense experience and of understanding could be answered through Lockean sensation.

Edwards also struggled with the problem of will, the source or spring of men's actions. The subject preoccupied him for the rest of his life. What, he asked, determines our actions? However suggestive, Locke again failed to supply adequate explanations. The Lockean notion that we are moved by mere uneasiness did not account for what Edwards believed to be the distinguishing mark of human consciousness, namely, the capacity to reflect upon what goes on in the mind itself. Whereas the animal, he said, has only "direct consciousness," or merely passive, involuntary consciousness, man is able to view himself contemplatively; he "was made for spiritual exercises and enjoyments, and therefore is made capable, by reflexion, to behold and contemplate spiritual things." "Hence," Edwards continued, "man is capable of Religion."[9]

The point to notice here is that from the outset Edwards inexorably linked religion and will. Or putting the matter differently, he pushed beyond Lockean psychology and into religion. Edwards' great contribution to epistemology, a contribution that he fully developed in his *Treatise Concerning Religious Affections,* published nearly thirty years later, finds its roots in this early insistence that contemplating things of the spirit determines in some way who we are and what we do. By contrast, the Lockean equation prescribed that perceiving through sensation governs our thought and action. Edwards in turn argued that action stems from will, which is itself determined by antecedent "spiritual exercises and enjoyments." As yet saying nothing about original sin or those motives eventuating in self-love, he asserted that the greatest of these exercises is the contemplation (the "mental existence") of Good, with no Lockean sensation necessarily associated with it. He elaborated this point by calling this mental existence the "mind's sense of Good" or, still further, "the greatest degree of apprehension, or perception, or idea" of Good. What, then, determines will, which later he will call religious affections? It is, he said, the "deepness" of this sense—"the clearness, liveliness and sensibleness, of the goodness; or the strength of the impression on the mind."[10] The terms are Lockean, the concept is not. For what Edwards tried to describe through the language of sensation is a dimension of existence that transcends sensation itself.

For the first time, he confronted the limitations of language. The frustration plagued him for years to come; his solution was his literary glory. Now concerned with this deepened sense of Good that determines the will, he formulated a key distinction between two kinds of knowledge of goodness. It is, he said, as between the person who "has just *tasted* honey, [and] has more of an idea of its goodness," and the person who "never tasted, though he also fully *believes* that it is very sweet, yes as sweet as it is."[11] The distinction is between a determining intuitive knowledge and a rational or speculative knowledge. The former enables a person to experience the illuminating power of divine excellence; the latter confines him to the natural world of substance and logic. The difference concerns the sense of the heart as distinct from speculative understanding.

What makes the *Notes* extraordinarily tantalizing is the emergence of certain patterns and strategies, reiterated in his "Miscellanies," that can be recognized as pointing towards Edwards' mature achievements.[12] Central to his development is this distinction between a purely intelligible understanding of truth and a taste of supernatural excellence. The distinction reinforces Professor Howard's argument that Edwards' mind "was obviously not operating as Locke's did." With far-reaching consequences Edwards saw the danger in placing too much reliance upon ratiocination. He cautioned that to go too far in abstractions was to risk clarity: "We had better stop a degree or two short of this . . . otherwise we shall be apt to run into error, and confound our minds." He realized the futility in depending upon strictly logical abstractions as a way to settle upon truth. He was not merely whimsical when he mused that "if we had perfect ideas of all things *at once,* that is, could have all in one view, we should know all truth at the same moment, and there would be no such thing as Ratiocination, or finding out Truth."[13]

The later entries in the *Notes* indicate that he was moving tantalizingly near such a "moment" in his own experience. That it occurred in 1723 he verifies in his autobiographical writings. There may be substance in Professor Howard's theory that in writing the *Notes* Edwards actually prepared the way for his own conversion. It seems certain that by the time he had put the manuscript aside he felt himself grasped by a new force that, according to his *Personal Narrative*, led to "a wonderful alternation" in his mind. It was, he said, "a sweet burning in my heart," a "ravishment," a "sweet complacency" in God's sovereignty, an acceptance of the "sweet and glorious" Calvinist doctrines (I,lxxxviii).

To understand this ravishment in Lockean terms was the task Edwards initially set for himself. No one has argued more authoritatively than Perry Miller the major influence of Locke in Edwards' intellectual development. Reading Locke's *Essay* was, says Miller, "the central and decisive event."[14] This judgment turned out to be both central and decisive in Miller's own interpretation of Edwards. Regardless of intellectual issues that show Edwards as anything but a strict Lockean, Miller insists that Edwards adopted Locke's sensational psychology "with the consistency that outdoes the modern 'behaviorist.' "[15] Accordingly, Edwards was "the first and most radical" of American empiricists.[16]

Whether or not we can agree with this estimation and with Miller's additional statement that Edwards actually read Locke "with ecstasy,"[17] there can be no doubt about the influence. What primarily interested Edwards was Locke's epistemology. One can imagine Edwards' initial security when, in light of his effort to obtain religious truth, he encountered Locke's answer to the question: From where do all the "materials" of reason and knowledge come? "To this I answer, in one word, from EXPERIENCE"[18] —*i.e.*, experience as registered on the mind, not as inherently belonging to it. That Edwards soon set up certain reservations about this theory did not reduce the initial impact. Ideas were thus made inseparable from sensational experience. They were the things made known through sensation. As Locke had said, "This great source of most of the ideas we have, depending wholly upon our senses, and derived by them to our understanding, I call SENSATION."[19]

The relevance to Christian epistemology was obvious. Unless a person experiences the love of God as a power from the outside that registers itself upon his mind, he cannot be said to know the idea of God's love. Ideas are authenticated only by experience. Of course Locke went on to claim that the mind is passive as it receives impressions.[20] Edwards' rejection of this claim pervades his entire work, grounded as it is upon the great paradox that God does all and man does all.[21] God's love is real when man's response is total. Locke also presupposed the phenomenon of cause (sensation) and effect (idea) to be according to nature. But Edwards never regarded religious experience as caused by "nature." For him God was neither nature nor a natural cause. He was infinite Being, a radically ontological God of love. Yet despite important differences in their thinking, Edwards did find in Locke's *Essay* the terms he needed to describe religious experience.

To say this is not to say, as Miller does, that Edwards was an empiricist. Granted that he was interested in speculating about the nature of religious experience and that Lockean sensationalism helped to explain it, but to suggest he read Locke "with ecstasy" confirms the disproportionate emphasis Miller gives to the Lockean influence. Of greater importance is the fact that Edwards read I Timothy 1:17 with ecstasy, preaching and writing all his life in Biblical and Calvinist language. Miller presses his argument dangerously far in claiming that empirical science shaped Edwards' essential method and point of view. This claim led Joseph Haroutunian in his review of Miller's *Jonathan Edwards* (1949) to say that "Professor Miller has done no justice to Edwards as a Christian thinker, as a man who, rightly or wrongly, thought of himself as expounding a life according to 'the excellency of Christ.' "[22] Haroutunian correctly asserts that Miller neglects the "supreme passion" of Edwards, namely, to know true virtue and holiness through Christ.

That Edwards was not a thoroughgoing empiricist is best seen in the nature of empiricism itself. The question arises whether empiricism can ever adequately treat religion. Empiricism as a scientific method calls for a certain scepticism, detachment, neutrality. The empiricist stands outside his subject in order to observe it dispassionately. Whether the object of his observation is the phenomenon of wind and tide or that of religious experience, his method requires sustained objectivity. Edwards was not an empiricist, unless as a child observing flying spiders and the color of rainbows. Even though his monumental *Treatise Concerning Religious Affections* purports to be a psychological study of religion, he cannot be considered a scientist (empiricist) in this field. The all-important fact is that his observations were subsumed into the more embracing category of religious conversion. This is the essential fact that fails to inform Miller's otherwise brilliant analysis. It is the same element missing in William James' *Varieties of Religious Experience,* written over 150 years after Edwards' great study and ostensibly treating the same subject.

In these Gifford Lectures given in Edinburgh in 1901-1902, James announced that this study of religious experience would rest upon empirical observations. What brought him to the study was the singular claim that "the religious propensities of man must be at least as interesting as any other of the facts pertaining to his mental constitution."[23] James intended his work to be a "descriptive survey," based upon what he called an "existential" point of view. But by this term he emphatically meant neither what the term implies today nor what it implies about Edwards. James meant simply that when one inquires into the existence of anything, the answer is given in *"an existential judgment* or proposition" rather than in an evaluative judgment. To him the phenomenon of religion existed as a blunt fact, and therefore his observations upon this phenomenon would be existential only in terms of this fact, without any necessary relationship to one's own private existence. Every religious phenomenon, James asserted, "has its history and its derivation from natural antecedents."[24]

To James this pattern applied to all religions, whether Buddhism, Christianity, or Islam. James said he would study religious phenomena "biologically and psychologically," though he confessed his real concern to be the pathological features as they are associated with religious "geniuses." With a singlemindedness to match any number of Nathaniel Hawthorne's fictional artists and scientists, James fastened upon those persons, including Edwards, who in their religious activity had manifested "acute fever," "symptoms of nervous instability," "abnormal psychical visitations," "exalted emotional sensibility," and all sorts of "exaggerations and perversions."[25] "Bent as we are," he announced, "on studying religion's existential conditions, we cannot possibly ignore these pathological aspects of the subject. We must describe and name them just as if they occurred in non-religious men."[26] Then announcing his full empirical position, even at the risk of disturbing his audience's sensibilities, he continued:

> It is true that we instinctively recoil from seeing an object to which our emotions and affections are committed handled by the intellect as any other object is handled. The first thing the intellect does with an object is to class it along with something else. But any object that is infinitely important to us and awakens our devotion feels to us also as if it must be *sui generis* and unique. Probably a crab would be filled with a sense of personal outrage if it could hear us class it without ado or apology as a crustacean, and thus dispose of it. "I am no such thing," it would say; "I am MYSELF, MYSELF alone."[27]

This is exactly the cry that filled Edwards' voice, as it did that of the Hebrew prophets, Paul, Augustine, Pascal, and Kierkegaard. John E. Smith, editor of Edwards' *Religious Affections,* asserts that "by no stretch of the imagination" was Edwards an existentialist, presumably in the sense that these other great voices were. Smith does acknowledge, however, that Edwards recognized that an understanding of religion which excludes first-person experience "is doomed to be lost in abstraction and to forfeit its relevance for religion."[28]

Definitions of existentialism need not detain us. The term is slippery almost to the point of unmanageableness. However, if we use the term not as a philosophy but as a way of philosophizing, we see its applicability to Edwards, whose way of knowing, distinguished by its Hebraic rather than Hellenic mode, reinforces the view that man is not merely part of a serene cosmic unity nor, as modern science declares, part of nature, but a unique being whose most characteristic utterance is indeed "MYSELF, MYSELF alone." The cry of man standing alone before God reverberates throughout Edwards' writing. It grows explicit when, as a text for one of his sermons, he quoted Ezekiel 22:14—"Can thine heart endure, or can thine hands be strong in the days that I shall deal with thee?"[29]

Thus in contrast with William James who took his viewpoint from outside the activity he was observing, Edwards stood firmly within it, within the theological circle of faith. From the beginning James followed the methods of Spinoza, whom he respectfully quoted: "I will analyze the actions and appetites of men as if it were a question of lines, of planes, and of solids."[30] Edwards, on the other hand, commenced his *Treatise Concerning Religious Affections* by quoting not Locke but I Peter 1:8: "Whom having not seen, ye love: in whom, though now ye see him not, yet believing, ye rejoice with joy unspeakable, and full of glory." The verbs describe Edwards' own involvement. Edwards was a Christian thinker, and the adjective makes all the difference. He wrote from within the full sense of the heart. His faith was like a grand cathedral. Standing outside, one sees no glory, nor can possibly imagine any; standing within, every ray of light reveals a harmony of unspeakable splendors. The metaphor, belonging to Hawthorne in *The Marble Faun* (ch. 33), captures the essence of Edwards' epistemology. Where he stood determined what he saw and knew.

CHAPTER TWO

Edwards and the Great Awakening

1
Loomings

Although starting with Locke, Edwards did not follow the broad
highway leading to David Hume, the Utilitarians, and Herbert Spen-
cer. The reason, said Perry Miller, was that he was "either too
profound or too unsophisticated."[1] Perhaps for the same curious
reason he did not go the way of the English Deists, even though his
intellectual master, Locke, had himself clearly marked the way in
The Reasonableness of Christianity in 1695 and John Toland had
broadened it the following year in *Christianity Not Mysterious*.
Edwards was attracted instead to the earlier Cambridge Platonists,
including such men as John Smith, John Owen, and Richard Sibbes,
who while preaching the reasonableness of religion also attached
importance to the mystery at the heart of the Christian faith. An
indebtedness to the rational mysticism of Plotinus infused their
idealism, which posited a universe "palpitating with spirit."[2]

What kept Edwards from being sidetracked by the British episte-
mologists who came after Locke was the mystery beyond the reasonableness of Christian faith. Thus Haroutunian claims that Edwards'
interest in philosophical speculation "disappeared with his youth,"
replaced by a deepening vision of godliness—"a sense of the glory of
the divine Being," Edwards wrote in his *Personal Narrative*—that was
to become *the* theme in his mature writing.[3] Miller, on the other
hand, speculates far less plausibly that it was the isolation of the
Connecticut Valley which "protected" Edwards from Hume and his
kind,[4] though Miller does add that Edwards had early been supplied
"by his religious nature with certain insights."[5] These insights pertained to nothing less than the mystery of Scripture and the sense of
divine glory they inspired within him.

Had Edwards been less than strangely altered, opportunities aplen-
ty were available for him to have taken a different theological course
even within the protective Connecticut Valley. Pervading all New

England was a vigorous liberalism stemming from what Herbert W. Schneider calls "a loss of the sense of sin."[6] Theocratic government had been undermined by all manner of social, political, and economic influence, not the least of which was that pernicious one called Yankee prosperity. The luxury and security provided by the larger towns deprived the later generations of the rigor that had sinewed the earlier community life. In ecclesiastical matters the strict Covenant of Grace that served as the unquestioned and professed basis for visible church membership had been ominously compromised, first by the Cambridge Platform of 1648 that permitted baptism to unprofessing children of the regenerate members, then by the Half-Way Covenant of 1662 that permitted even the children of *un*professing members to be baptized. Although the 1662 ruling had not allowed these unprofessing members to partake of the Holy Communion, Connecticut Valley's own Solomon Stoddard cleared away this restriction in the publication of *The Doctrine of Instituted Churches* (1700), his purpose being to show that the sacrament was not a privilege reserved for the regenerate but rather a *means* of salvation open to the unregenerate. For the complete triumph of liberalism nothing more was needed after Stoddard's *coup de grâce* than the revolutionary arguments concerning democratic church government that John Wise supplied in his influential *Vindication of the Government of the New England Churches* (1717). No longer, Wise argued, should civil society take its model from the theocratic principles of the church. The tables must be turned, the Puritan philosophy of the Holy Commonwealth reversed, so that the church would be obliged to follow the democratic model of civil society. The consequence of this victory for the laity and for secular democracy, says Schneider, was nothing less than "the dethronement of God."[7] In terms which the prosperous Bostonian greeted and the Calvinist Edwards abhorred, society was rejecting the sense of the heart for that of the purse.

For all its frontier isolation, Northampton offered Edwards no protection against these conditions. Not only was the community one of the largest and most prosperous in the colony, and one proud of its morality, reputation, and culture, but from the very pulpit that the "sickly, scholarly youth"[8] now occupied had come Stoddard's message of liberalism heard round the countryside for over twenty years. The obvious highway for Edwards to have taken was the one mapped out by Stoddard. Even the equally venerable Cotton Mather, who died the year before Stoddard, afforded subtle alternatives to the tortuous Calvinism that was Edwards' way. Mather had earlier opposed the compromised view of the Lord's Supper as "effectual means" of salvation, but in later years he set forth his own self-evident liberalism in such works as *Reasonable Religion* (1700), *Bonifacius, or Essays to Do Good* (1710), *Reason Satisfied and Faith Established* (1712), and *The Christian Philosopher* (1721). In one way or another all these works illumined the ever broadening avenue of American eighteenth-century thought. There was, then, no "safety" for the eighteenth-century Calvinist, even for one who knew his Locke and Newton. Nor is there any pragmatic accounting for Edwards' compulsion to travel the other road that was to be marked by experiences unbeknown to persons closest to him.

Edwards' security came from a Calvinism that his own spiritual hunger, anxiety, and joy had authenticated and that, in turn, had provided the doctrinal basis for his theology of the heart. Chief among its tenets was God's absolute sovereignty. Edwards had no sympathy for the popular view that God and man were somehow, as it were, on a see-saw: as man goes up in common sense and resourcefulness, God must therefore go down. If anything, the reverse was true. The real truth, however, was not in such an image at all. God is infinite, man is finite, and thus the difference between the two is an infinite one. The only mediation is through Christ. Man is totally dependent on the Son of God for all his wisdom, righteousness, and redemption. Let all men who appear "eminent in holiness, and abundant in good works" hear the truth: there is "an absolute and universal dependence of the redeemed on God for all their good"; and God hereby "is exalted and glorified in the work of redemption" (II,7, 2-3).

Edwards preached these words in Boston on July 8, 1731, exactly ten years to the day before he delivered his famous Enfield sermon about sinners in the hands of an angry God. In this Boston sermon, "God Glorified in Man's Dependence," Edwards could hardly have been more explicit in identifying his audience. He chose a text from Paul's letter to the Corinthians who, Edwards reflected, lived but a short distance from Athens, "for many ages the most famous seat of philosophy and learning in the world." Did not those persons now sitting before Edwards see Harvard in much the same light? Edwards did not need to ask the question. Did not the doctrines of God's absolute sovereignty and man's absolute dependence seem foolishness to the liberal Harvard clergy? Again Edwards did not need to ask. For all he left unsaid, the sermon was clearly "a gage to battle, a challenge to combat"; it brought "new fervor in preaching"; it "was as significant in Edwards' life and in the history of New England theology as when Schleiermacher preached his discourse upon the same subject, which marks the date of the ecclesiastical reaction of the nineteenth century."[9] Let there be no mistake about the position I will henceforth take, Edwards said in effect. The doctrines I will preach are living and intoxicating because they arise from experiential knowledge. Supreme among these doctrines is the one affirming an inscrutable, immutable Deity for adoration, not for mere speculation. Let us never forget that our relationship with the Deity, who is under no obligation to us, is at best a relationship of dependence, regardless of what our works and reason say to the contrary.

Not for another century would America have a spokesman equal in vision to Edwards—or, more accurately, a seer who would depict the full and terrible consequences when man forgets the nature of this relationship. Nor would there be anyone better able to describe the Calvinist minister's austere responsibility for preaching this truth. That person was Herman Melville, whose fictional Father Mapple conceived his clerical duty in terms no less resolute than did Edwards as he stood before his Boston audience:

> Woe to him [spoke Father Mapple] who this world charms from Gospel duty! Woe to him who seeks to pour oil upon the waters when God has brewed them into a gale! Woe to him who seeks to please rather than to appal! Woe to him whose good name is more to him than goodness! Woe to him who, in this world, courts not dishonor! Woe to him who would not be true, even though to be false were salvation. Yea, woe to him who, as the great Pilot Paul has it, while preaching to others is himself a castaway! (*Moby Dick*, ch. 8)

Within the next month Edwards' sermon was printed—his first published writing—for all New England to read. Prefacing it was an "Advertisement to the Reader" written by the Rev. William Cooper and Thomas Prince, Jr., who with understandable motives expressed delight in their having witnessed such a youthful preacher "pitching upon so noble a subject"; here, they said, "was the very soul of piety" (II,2). Indeed it was. But little did they realize that this sermon was the prelude to a great battle, one that for all the woe it would bring to Edwards would never bring him the soul-destroying woe spoken of by Melville's Father Mapple. Edwards' ever deepening insights were too secure for that.

Before the tempest broke, Edwards delivered two other sermons that were doctrinally as important for his religion of the heart as his Boston sermon on the sovereignty of God. One was "A Divine and Supernatural Light," preached in the summer of 1733 and published the following year. The other, a two-sermon series preached in 1734, was entitled "Justification by Faith Alone," expanded and published four years later as one of the treatises in *Five Discourses on Important Subjects.* No sermon contains more of the essential Edwards than does "A Divine and Supernatural Light." Perry Miller does not exaggerate in saying that within this sermon "the whole of Edwards' system is contained in miniature."[10] The other discourse, on justification by faith, further strengthened his doctrinal position.

In the 1733 sermon Edwards argued two essential points. One concerned the difference between natural and regenerate man; the other pertained to the divine and supernatural light, a metaphor for grace and divine reality. These points combined into Edwards' most celebrated statement on the subject of religious knowledge. Clearly distinct from Locke, Edwards asserted that religious knowledge was of a different order from knowledge that consists of sense data that register upon the mind of natural man. Edwards did not rule out the possibility that such sense "impressions" strangely quicken the imagination. In fact he granted, as did Calvin, the importance of other natural capacities, including conscience and reason.[11] But contrary to Locke, Edwards presupposed that in all knowledge, including religious knowledge, the natural faculties "are not merely passive, but are active" (II,15). In religious knowledge man does all, he responds totally; yet what he does is nothing compared with the indispensable and absolute prior initiative of God.

A radical and qualitative difference separates the natural and the regenerate man. That difference consists not in the quantitative enlargement of natural man's knowledge but in the gulf that separates this knowledge from what Edwards called "a real sense and apprehension of the divine excellency . . . a spiritual and saving conviction of the truth and reality of these things" (II,14). Because natural man knows God only as object, he has no apprehension, no sense of the glory of God. Through reason he may construct proofs of God's existence and call it natural theology. He may, as Emil Brunner more recently has suggested, posit divine excellency as an objective reality within natural man's possibility to know (except as prevented by sin) and then, if such knowledge eventuates, call it general revelation.[12] But unlike Brunner and more like Karl Barth, Edwards insisted not only that this light of grace and divine reality is special, insofar as it is mediated only through Jesus Christ, but also that this light is personal and saving. To Edwards, God is a living, personal God; man is a unique personality; and through grace the regenerate man knows that this divine-human relationship is a "saving" one.

The question arises whether this radical difference between the natural man, who stands in a remote and impersonal relationship with an objective God, and the regenerate man, who has a sense of God in his heart, means that this divine light is everything, that the old Saul ceased to exist when the new Paul was born on the Damascus road, that natural man is not only weak but dead. The question is as stark as that between death and life. Edwards did not compromise, nor did he preach a kind of flexibility that would mitigate the significance of rebirth. Instead he stretched the paradox to its offensive extreme by insisting upon the concept of immediacy: that a spiritual and divine light, "*immediately* imparted to the soul by God*," is different from any that is obtained by natural means (II,13, my italics). At first the term "immediately" may suggest only a point of time, an instant. Thus during the great revivals that soon were to sweep through the Connecticut Valley persons testified to immediate experiences of salvation, as if within the blinking of an eye they were somehow reborn. Edwards took great pains to minimize the experience of the Enthusiasts who made such claims of instantaneous regeneration. In "The Divine and Supernatural Light" he cautioned that sheer sentiment or emotion is not evidence of the true light. That many people are "greatly affected" by things of religion was no sure sign, he said, that they were still anything but "wholly graceless." Yet Edwards did affirm the mighty drama of conversion and strove mightily to distinguish the real drama from its deceptive counterpart.

When Edwards spoke of the divine light as being "immediately imparted," he was referring first to the qualitative nature of this light and second to the occurrence of the event in time. In short, Edwards' concern was with epistemology before chronology. The primary meaning of immediacy thus comes in the unmitigated distinction (1) between natural and spiritual knowledge, and (2) between the speculative and intuitive means to it. Natural knowledge is devoid of special revelation. That natural knowledge may represent a primordial consciousness or a vastly higher level of reason does not imply a still further evolutionary process that finally leads to religious truth. Despite a finely-honed speculative faculty, natural man cannot "achieve" spiritual knowledge for the profoundly simple reason that such knowledge, instead of being reached by man, is given, imparted, revealed by God. Natural man does not finally grasp it, as if it were the prize waiting at the end of strenuous thinking or morally upright living. Rather than grasping it, regenerate man is grasped by it. Furthermore, if an impact can be said to occur upon the soul at such an event, it is not the impact of natural truth like that which we experience when we learn the law of gravity or $E=MC^2$. It is instead the impact of revealed divine truth that infuses the heart and engenders commitment.

Even though spiritual struggle accompanied Edwards' hard-won insights and deepening meanings, he never portrayed the drama of conversion in any other way but to highlight the role of God as the divine initiator of revelation and grace. Only after Edwards posited the sovereignty of God's role did he address himself to the human situation. As will be shown in a later chapter, he described man's condition in highly dramatic terms, none more effective than the term "immediacy." We have said that the term meant the immediate juxtaposition of nature and grace, darkness and light. No intervening institutions like churches and universities could blur this unequivocal distinction. Neither teacher nor clergyman, reason nor philosophical systems, principalities nor powers, could come in the way to modify these separate conditions of existence. But the term also meant the immediate *now*, the existential moment for each man as he stands in a state of "darkness and delusion" or "holiness and grace" (II,14). With startling insight Edwards dramatized hell or heaven as a condition of *this* moment, and neither distance nor time separated man from its coercive urgency. For all the preparatory study, reflection, philanthropy, and prayer that man engages in, "that work of grace upon the soul whereby a person is brought out of a state of total corruption and depravity into a state of grace, to an interest in Christ, and to be actually a child of God, is in a moment."[13] Just as the truth of Abraham's fear and trembling became real for Kierkegaard only at the immediate moment when he experienced a sense of it in his heart, so also did Edwards realize the truth of divine illumination only when it became an immediate event in *his* heart. He expected nothing less from his Northampton parishioners.

At such a moment reason is also sanctified. Objections to the offense that common sense finds implicit in Christian mysteries are overcome. The divine light "positively helps reason" to accept the very reasonableness of the light and its sovereign, saving immediacy (II,14). Unsanctified or natural reason, having only the capacity to infer by argument and proposition, cannot perceive this light. Only within the province of the heart can this perception occur. When reason is thus brought within this totally integrating province, it enables one to see the excellency of those doctrines that are the subject matter of this light or knowledge. Sanctified reason penetrates to the divine congruity to which natural man is blind.

Rebelliousness toward apparent absurdity changes to trust in what sanctified reason now finds as God's order. This trust is total openness to God's reasonable will in which, Edwards said, we find our peace. Dante before him and T. S. Eliot after him said as much. His New England parishioners did not. Such an idea was vaguely at cross-purposes with what was dawning in the American consciousness as a more beguiling independence and cultural identity. Already the stirrings of liberalism were shaping an emerging American personality that would find its expression not in Edwards' theology nor Melville's sombre artistry but in Emerson and Whitman, whose visions of limitless human possibility embraced self-trust above all.

2
Justification by Faith Alone

With Edwards' sermons on justification by faith alone the first indications of trouble appeared. His earlier Boston sermon, after all, had been only the single performance of a youthful minister; and his one on "Divine and Supernatural Light" had through its eloquence made palatable an otherwise perilous doctrine. But there could be no doubt that in the incessant severity of this doctrine of justification Edwards meant business. Clearly he was beginning to set a pace that would prove too demanding for his congregation, and to preach about a divine authority that squared less and less with the American sense of independence.

Edwards realized the difficulty of his text, Romans 4:5—"But to him that worketh not, but believeth on him that justifieth the ungodly, his faith is counted for righteousness." Rendered in his own words, the doctrine loomed large and forbidding: "That we are justified by faith in Christ, and not by any manner of virtue or goodness of our own" (I,622). He acknowledged that many in his congregation would call such an assertion "absurd," finding in it "a great deal of ignorance" and much "inconsistence" (I,622). In asking "every one's patience" to hear him out, he knew only too well, as he wrote in his later Preface, that he was now throwing into jeopardy what many had been taught since their infancy, namely, that their good works, obedience, and virtue qualified them for reward. Edwards' contrary doctrine caused "unusual ruffle," and he candidly admitted that he had been "greatly reproached" for preaching it and had suffered "open abuse." But he would be put off by neither the complexity nor the harsh consequences of the doctrine. Furthermore, *this* doctrine was "the very bottom stone" in the construction of his argument against liberalism (I,646). Let the Arminians be satisfied with simplifications and let them render hard truths harmless and comfortable. Granted that Christian doctrines may contain "something easy"; yet, said Edwards, "they also contain great mysteries," worthy of the closest intellectual diligence, accuracy, and distinctions, as well as the most honest if painful confrontation. Again, the demands that Edwards placed upon himself he also placed upon his parishioners. He was convinced that if religion meant anything it meant everything.

The doctrine of justification itself posed no difficulties. Its meaning was simply that in justification we are (1) approved of God as free from the guilt of sin and its punishment and (2) blessed with that righteousness that brings us into communion with all believers. Justification means the remission of sin (deliverance from hell) and the inheritance of eternal life (the purchase of heaven). The difficulty comes in the word "by": justification *by* faith alone. Is faith the prerequisite for the justification that supposedly follows? Is faith like an instrument that God uses to perform the act of justification? Is Christ alone the condition for our justification and salvation? Are other qualifications and actions like loving our brethren and forgiving them their trespasses conditions of justification? What is the difference between justification by faith and by law? Recognizing the problems, Edwards made one point clear at the outset: for us Christ "purchased justification by his blood" (I,624). The centrality Edwards gave to Christ is never more emphatic than at this point; it provides the basis for Edwards' conception of faith.

Edwards affirmed that Christian faith consists of man's total response to Christ. To "have" faith is to be in Christ, as members are to the head and branches to the stalk. Faith is union. Edwards held that only as we are first united in Christ will we be justified by God. The sequence is all-important: "Our being in him is the ground of our being accepted [justified] " (I,625). Justification by faith is the same as justification-by-our-being-in-Christ. Union in Christ is not the reward of faith; union *is* faith. Furthermore, man actively gives himself to this union. Edwards held that faith is "the soul's *active* uniting with Christ"; Christ who first came to man now treats man as "capable of act and choice" to come to him. "Such faith," said Calvin, "does not merely believe about Christ; it embraces him with the soul."[14]

The crux of the doctrine specifies that union with Christ is not the reward for faith but is faith, and that by faith *alone* we are justified. To suppose, for instance, that God grants this relationship with Christ as a reward for good works is inconsistent with one's being under condemnation until he comes into the relationship. The same inconsistency obtains when a person expects to be justified before he first unites with Christ. In both instances, Edwards emphatically attacked any notion that elevated human merit as the prior condition for God's act. According to the tenor of the Covenant of Works, a person was to be accepted and rewarded only for work's sake; but in the Covenant of Grace the work is accepted and rewarded only for the person's sake. In bringing new life to this nonlegalistic Covenant of Grace, Edwards struck at the foundations of New England Covenant Theology, which for generations had favored the logic of works, until by Edwards' day such logic virtually demanded God's concessions to works alone.[15]

Perry Miller attempts to show that Edwards' interpretation of justification by faith owed much to "his inspired reading of Newton."[16] Determined to keep Edwards an empiricist, whether Lockean or Newtonian, Miller argues that the root of the doctrine of justification is Newton's concept "of an antecedent to a subsequent, in which the subsequent, when it does come to pass, proves to be whatever it is by itself and in itself, without determination by the precedent." "All effects," Miller continues, "must therefore have their causes, but no effect is a 'result' of what has gone before."[17] Edwards' theological argument that the rewardableness of good works is not antecedent to justification but follows it is supposedly analogous to Newton's insight. Whatever Edwards owed to Newton, his greater debt is to Paul, whom he quoted prolifically throughout the treatise, at no time with more telling effect than when he cited Galatians 2:20: "I am crucified with Christ: nevertheless I live; yet not I, but Christ liveth in me: and the life which I now live in the flesh I live by the faith of the Son of God, who loved me, and gave himself for me" (I,642).

Behind the doctrine of justification Miller finds an essential awesomeness, an inner connection of cause and effect that is "mysterious and terrifying," a hidden power resembling what in nature holds the atoms in cohesion and operates in gravity. But Miller presses his Newtonian analogy beyond its metaphorical limits, allowing Newton, as it were, to swallow Edwards. Unlike Edwards, Miller fails to take into account an essential love. To Miller the "dark forces of nature" deep behind Newton's façade of rationalism are more mysterious than anything the Christian insight affords. His analogy between these "dark forces" and the God who violates human logic in the act of justification breaks down when Miller claims that these natural forces overshadow the "dazzling glare" of Calvinist predestination. In short, the greater power belongs to nature and not to God, a conclusion that misses the very core of Edwards' thought. For it was always God as the supremely "wise being," the one who "delights in order" and whose justification of man in Christ was "a testimony of his love of order," that Edwards held to be the "first foundation" of all reality (I,627). Moreover, it was God as love who, in Edwards' orthodox view, brought man by faith into divine coherence. Thus man's works do not serve a legalistic covenant that promises rewards for obedience but instead "are works of that faith that worketh by love: and every such act of obedience, wherein it is inward, and the act of the soul, is only a new effective act of reception of Christ, and adherence to the glorious Savior" (I,642).

The importance of this doctrine for what was looming on the New England scene received no better testimony than Edwards' own Preface written in 1738. In spite of the abuse he suffered for preaching the sermons on justification, he declared his vindication. For soon afterward, in the autumn of 1734, "God's work wonderfully brake forth amongst us, and souls began to flock to Christ, as the Savior in whose righteousness alone they hoped to be justified" (I,620). The Great Awakening had begun, and American religious thought and practice would not be the same again. In Frank Hugh Foster's opinion, the theological movement begun by Edwards when he preached these specific sermons "acquired an importance for the whole Christian civilization when it became the molding force of a great part of the constructive religious work done in the United States of America."[18] If this judgment is hyperbolic, there is solid validity in Edwards' own statement that "this was the doctrine on which this work [the Great Awakening] in its beginning was founded, as it evidently was in the whole progress of it" (I,620).

3

The Effulgent Connecticut Valley

The doctrine of justification *sola fide* points toward the great doctrine of predestination. What the former teaches about God's relation to the person in Christ applies also to what the latter teaches about God's relation to his people. The first has to do with the individual, the second with history. Both concern God's redemptive work. Both presuppose a sovereign God of power, grace, and love, whom to know is to receive the spiritual fruits of joy and peace. Yet both doctrines also teach that God's action, though it can be apprehended, can never be fully understood. There is no comprehensible explanation of God's ways in justification, for man's prior works count as nothing. Neither is there a deterministic logic, a cause and effect, to account for God's ways in history. Nevertheless in the fabric of both doctrines is the certainty that nothing God does is fortuitous—mysterious, yes, but never apart from divine intention. This certainty is arrived at by fixing one's heart and mind upon Scripture, Christ, and the history of God's people. These things Edwards preached with his own keen fixedness.

Religious experience seized individuals and community alike. By 1735 all Northampton was caught up in what Edwards regarded as God's redemptive work. By the next year revivalism had spread to South Hadley, Suffield, Sunderland, Deerfield, Hatfield, West Springfield, Long Meadow, Enfield, Westfield, Northfield, East Windsor, Coventry, Stratford, Ripton, Tolland, Hebron, Bolton, Woodbury. God indeed was moving in strange, mysterious, and rapid ways. As for Northampton, where for several years after Stoddard's death a certain "dullness in religion" had set in, including not a little "night-walking, and frequenting the tavern, and lewd practices" (FN,146),[19] approximately 300 souls were now brought to Christ within a single year.

These were the facts Edwards reported in *A Faithful Narrative of the Surprising Work of God in the Conversion of Many Hundred Souls in Northampton, and the Neighboring Towns and Villages* (1737). But this account, an enlargement of the "Narrative of Surprising Conversions" which Edwards had sent to the Rev. Benjamin Colman in Boston the previous year, is far more than mere factual history. Written within the context of his own personal conversion and in many ways anticipating his *Personal Narrative,* this 1737 document signals the first time Edwards came to grips with the phenomenon of religious experience on a mass scale. Already indebted to Lockean psychology, he now saw himself as a clinical witness to God's work in the conversion of others. Moreover, he beheld a dramatic corroboration of doctrinal justification, plus hints that the revival itself was but an episode in a supra-historical sphere to be known to the elect as salvation history. Criticism frequently calls attention to the bizarre features of what occurred in Northampton. In later writings Edwards sought to correct this impression without repudiating *A Faithful Narrative*. He was convinced that these conversions—sudden, dramatic, inexplicable—were related to God's "peculiar and immediate work" in this chosen town (*FN*, 210). For the present he was satisfied to describe them. Later he attempted to make them theologically understandable. The task summoned his greatest powers. Ironically it also laid the groundwork for his personal tragedy. For the intellectual vindication that he structured belied the singularly self-authenticating sense of the heart. To make visible whether in treatises or institutions what is invisible must fail, all the more notably when the visible takes forms of hard and rigid outline.

As a description of the Northampton revival, *A Faithful Narrative* has an impressive dramatic form which helps account for the fact that during Edwards' lifetime it was printed in full at least sixty times—ten times in five countries and three languages.[20] In the opening section Edwards provides the setting, observing that the people of Northampton were as "sober, and orderly, and good" as any in New England, and adding that "they are as rational and understanding a people as most I have been acquainted with" (*FN*, 144-145). It was, however, their smugness about religion that Edwards found disconcerting. What suddenly shook them into new sobriety were two deaths in nearby Pascommuck in April 1734, one of a young man who died of pleurisy after two days of delirium, the other of a young woman who before she died was "considerably exercised in mind" about the state of her soul. Stirred by these solemn events, plus an ever threatening Arminianism which some people interpreted as the sign that God was withdrawing from the land, the townspeople were further unsettled in December by the startling conversion of several persons, especially that of a young woman considered one of the "greatest company-keepers in the whole town" (*FN*, 149). God had given her "a new heart, truly broken and sanctified" (*FN*, 149). Soon others were likewise affected, until by the spring and summer of 1735 "the town seemed to be full of the presence of God: it never was so full of love, nor so full of joy; and yet so full of distress, as it was then" (*FN*,151). Parents rejoiced over their children as newborn, husbands over their wives, and wives over their husbands. When neighboring villagers came to see what was happening, they too were affected. The Valley had become spiritually alive, and within Northampton alone, a town of some 200 families, approximately 300 souls were saved.

After describing these initial and more general occurrences, Edwards concentrates upon the specific manifestations of the conversion experiences. What he is driven to understand is the relation between the invisible action of God's spirit and the visible effects. His certainty that a relationship existed intensified the whole drama of salvation.

Among his newly awakened parishioners Edwards noted, first, their sudden misery over what they saw as their sinful condition. Their consciences were "smitten," he wrote, "as if their hearts were pierced through with a dart" (*FN*,160). Convinced of their sin, they sometimes experienced "awful apprehensions" about the true depth of corruption in which they existed, sometimes fear that their sins were unpardonable, and always a "terrifying sense" of their total condition. The second phase brought a conviction that God is just in condemning them. With this they could scarcely forbear crying out, " 'Tis just! 'Tis just!" (*FN*,170). The third phase was one of calmness that followed their sense of all-sufficient grace. Their thoughts now were fixed on God and his "sweet and glorious attributes" (*FN*,171). They longed to have communion with Christ. There was wrought in them "a holy repose of soul," a new and lively sense of the heart (*FN*,173). Those persons most confounded were the town's intellectuals, who became like "mere babes" who knew nothing. For everyone the experience was "all new and strange," sometimes releasing laughter, tears, or loud weeping. For everyone the manner of God's work on the soul was like a dawning light:

> In some, converting light is like a glorious brightness suddenly shining in upon a person, and all around him: they are in a remarkable manner brought out of darkness into marvellous light. In many others it has been like the dawning of the day, when at first but a little light appears, and it may be is presently hid with a cloud; and then it appears again, and shines a little brighter, and gradually increases, with intervening darkness, till at length, perhaps, it breaks forth more clearly from behind the clouds. (*FN*,177-178)

With great fervor Edwards brought his account to a climax by describing in near day-by-day detail the conversion of Abigail Hutchinson, followed by an account of four-year-old Phebe Bartlet and her spectacular conversion. The first sketch is the more compelling one, even with its shades of sentimentalism. In this sketch Edwards recounts the last seven months of Abigail's life, starting with a certain Monday in December of 1734 when her brother first told her about the young, "company-keeping" woman who had been converted to God. Edwards follows the unmarried and sickly Abigail through the three stages described previously, ending with the convergence of religious vision and death. Little Phebe, on the other hand, lived to old age. Edwards' account of her childhood conversion became famous throughout New England,[21] especially the part describing the long hours in her closet, where she prayed to God for salvation and presumably saw all manner of awesome visions. Unaffected by her mother's efforts to calm her and subjected to horrendous spells of weeping, little Phebe woefully confessed, "Yes, I am afraid I shall go to hell!" (FN,200). When she emerged from her same closet at a later time, she exclaimed, "I can find God now . . . I love God . . . now I shan't [go to hell] " (FN,200-201).

Easy as it is to dismiss the story of Phebe, it offers, like the account of Abigail, a clue to the far-reaching dimension with which Edwards interpreted these episodes. If, as he believed, the Northampton revival was part of God's larger redemptive work in history, then the drama of these two souls assumes importance far beyond that of individual case studies. These two accounts also reveal Edwards' sensitivity to the psychological implications of religious experience, even among children. Little Phebe became a prototype for certain children in nineteenth-century American fiction whose intelligence borders the frightening and forbidden domain of the supernatural, whether for good or evil. According to F. O. Matthiessen, Nathaniel Hawthorne's portrayal of Pearl in The Scarlet Letter reflects something of the "terrifying precocity" which Edwards' dialectic of feelings revealed in children who underwent the emotional strain of the Great Awakening.[22] Certain of Henry James' fictional children bear the marks of a similar inheritance.

The religious intensity in Northampton could not be sustained indefinitely. What brought it to sombre subsidence was the fate of

Edwards' uncle, Joseph Hawley, whose spiritual travail had taken him into desperate melancholy. According to Edwards, the devil quickly seized this advantage to drive Hawley into ever more "despairing thoughts," leading to sleeplessness, delirium, and finally suicide on June 1, 1735. For the sake of other citizens' well-being, the subsidence fortunately prevailed, even though immediately after Hawley had slit his throat other people in the town were sufficiently upset to have claimed to hear voices bidding them, " 'Cut your own throat, now is a good opportunity: *now, NOW!*" (*FN,*207). Such hysteria, however, in no way dissuaded Edwards from his belief that God had truly visited the community. He wrote as a denouement that God had made the citizens of Northampton into "a new people" through the "great and marvellous work of conversion and sanctification" (*FN,*209). Echoing the words of destiny uttered over a hundred years earlier by Boston's John Winthrop, Edwards now envisioned Northampton as *the* city "set upon a hill" (*FN,*210).

However low Northampton's fires of revivalism burned after the Hawley incident, Edwards' *A Faithful Narrative* served as a popular handbook to keep them alive elsewhere. As for Edwards' parish, one could hardly say it returned to its former "dullness." In 1736 work started on a new church building that Edwards dedicated on Christmas the following year. In 1739 he preached a series of important sermons on the theology of history, published posthumously in Edinburgh as a *History of the Work of Redemption* (1774). In 1740 the English revivalist George Whitefield visited Northampton and other towns and cities, and once again the fervor quickened, this time bringing manifestations even more bizarre than the earlier ones. Within the austere walls of New England churches congregations bewailed their sins aloud and groaned in fear and repentance. Whitefield's departure after only a month's itinerary left ample room for such New Lights as James Davenport, Samuel Hopkins, Samuel Buell, Gilbert Tennent, and Edwards' pupil Joseph Bellamy to keep the fires of hell plainly visible before the people. Edwards' own Enfield sermon in 1741, the most famous he ever preached and the most celebrated in all American history, belonged to this brief climax of the Great Awakening.

Amid the religious fury, Edwards not only wrote his deeply spiritual autobiography, the *Personal Narrative,* but sought to maintain an objectivity regarding the tumult raging all around him. No less alarmed by the denunciations than by the public excesses, he wrote two treatises in the hope that both would serve to answer the Old Lights—the rationalists and liberals who were denouncing revivalism—and also to temper the Enthusiasts who were distorting its visible marks. The first treatise appeared in 1741 bearing the title, *The Distinguishing Marks of a Work of the Spirit of God, Applied to that uncommon Operation that has lately appeared on the Minds of many of the People of This Land.* Earlier the same year, this work had been delivered in shorter form as a sermon to faculty and students at Yale College. The second treatise, worthy to be considered a major work, was published in March 1743. It carried the title *Some Thoughts Concerning the present Revival of Religion in New England, And the Way in which it ought to be acknowledged and promoted.*

Reading these two works helps one understand the difficulty Edwards faced during the Awakening. On the one hand he knew better than anyone else that religious experience is never wholly pure, entirely spiritual, and totally free from the "natural and carnal." He uttered his own denunciations against those persons who believed fainting, bodily tremors, and all manner of natural passion to be indispensable elements in religious conversion. He realized the advantages such behavior brought to anti-revivalists like Charles Chauncy and Solomon Williams in their case against what Edwards considered the true even if extraordinary circumstances of God's work. In short, he knew that the marks of the Spirit may be visible but also deceptive. On the other hand, he hated religious lukewarmness. Far better, he thought, to have religion the main business of life than to have life in Northampton consist mainly of business. Religion that is vital compels the total man, even if his subsequent response leads to imprudences and irregularities. "We are to consider," he said, "that the end for which God pours out his Spirit, is to make men holy, and not to make them politicians" (*Distinguishing Marks,* 241). A thousand imprudences would not disprove an action to be of the Spirit of God. Edwards noted that the New Testament church of Corinth, blessed with large measures of God's Spirit, also displayed "manifold imprudences" at the Lord's Supper and in the exercise of church affairs.[23] In a similar way the New

Englanders who were truly touched by God sometimes displayed the worst kind of vehemence. Facing these coexisting extremes, Edwards defended revivalism in its full visibility.

Edwards yielded no ground when the attack came from Charles Chauncy, co-pastor of Boston's First Church. It is true that Edwards was critical of some of the same things Chauncy was. Both men condemned the type of revivalism that led to spiritual pride, disregard for the external order of worship and prayer, the censuring of other persons, and the kind of immediate inspiration that supposedly validated lay exhorting. These criticisms Chauncy consolidated and set forth in his *Seasonable Thoughts on the State of Religion in New England* (1743), a work that he hoped would discredit Edwards' theology of the heart once and for all. For in addition to attacking irregular behavior as inconsistent with Christian conduct, Chauncy also charged that emotionalism had little if any connection with Christian doctrine. The real issue behind Chauncy's attack was his advocacy of reason and common sense. But Edwards knew that an even deeper issue was at stake, namely, Chauncy's effort to close the gap between such distinctions as regenerate and unregenerate, sacred and secular, spiritual and natural, holy love and moral legalism. Because Edwards recognized this as the basic theological issue in New England, he steadfastly defended revivalism even with its excrescences.

Edwards had no illusions about man's condition. Almost plaintively he cried, "What a poor, blind, weak, and miserable creature is man, at his best estate!" (*Thoughts,* 495). But Edwards also had no doubts about God's saving work. As he made clear in both treatises written during the stormy revival, God's extraordinary work bears relation to the extraordinary events. Even though a work of the Spirit cannot always be judged by its visible effects, yet such effects may be related to the Spirit's work. Edwards supported this logic with a plethora of Biblical references. He also argued that certain physical signs serve as a language, perhaps more efficacious in conveying a sense of God's power than the language of words. Apparent imprudences may be such legitimate means of expression.

Yet Edwards cautiously refused to get trapped by what he considered the minor considerations of tears, groans, and agonizing outcries. If, as Edwards said, Christ had thought it necessary for the church's sake, he would have given ministers instructions for dealing with such matters; he "would have told 'em how the pulse should beat under such and such religious exercises of mind; when men should look pale, and when they should shed tears" (*Thoughts,* 300). We should not be surprised that such effects do occur. Human nature "that is as the grass, a shaking leaf, a weak withering flower" might indeed totter under such glory as is God's (*Thoughts,* 302). We cannot forget Jeremiah's outcry (4:19): "My bowels, my bowels! I am pained at my very heart: my heart maketh a noise in me; I cannot hold my peace, because thou hast heard, O my soul, the sound of the trumpet, the alarm of war." Or that of Habakkuk (1:16): "When I heard, my belly trembled; my lips quivered at the voice." Indeed New England's cup had also overflowed. Yet, Edwards refused to be sidetracked from his essential point—that what Scripture teaches is divinity, not anatomy. He did not allow New Englanders to forget that God works in men's lives. God's saving influence is manifested when people confess Christ as the Son of God, when they have greater regard for Scripture, when they see the divine and supernatural light of truth and respond to the spirit of love. In short, when Edwards declared that these marks relate to holy affections which have their seat chiefly in the heart, he was reiterating his own discovery of twenty years earlier and anticipating his great treatise to be published in 1746.

In these earlier treatises Edwards offered no more positive sign of God's glorious work than the religious experience of his wife Sarah. Here is not another Abigail or Phebe but someone close to his own life and religious experience. Sarah was not a new convert, her original conversion having occurred "twenty-seven years" earlier, long before the great enthusiasm had begun and, Edwards added, before Mr. Whitefield and Mr. Tennent had set to work. Such too could be said for the onset of her more recent experience, originating prior to the Northampton revival of 1735. Edwards' remarkable account included descriptions of Sarah's physical state while her soul dwelled with God: she was deprived "of all ability to stand or speak; sometimes the hands were clinched, and the flesh cold, but the senses still remaining" (*Thoughts,* 332). Her emotions ranged from the dread over an eternal hell to the sweet peace of spiritual serenity. The account is a great paean, a mighty apologetic, that concludes in an unforgettable outburst: "Now if such things are enthusiasm, and the fruits of a distempered brain, let my brain be evermore possessed of that happy distemper! If this be distraction, I pray God that the world of mankind may all be seized with this benign, meek, beneficent, beatifical, glorious distraction!" (*Thoughts,* 341). Here was eloquence that soared above the safe and prudent reasonings of the Arminians. To ears grown dull to such talk his words were like the piercing notes of a solitary trumpet.

The importance of the Great Awakening to Edwards cannot be overemphasized. To him the revivals sweeping up and down the Connecticut Valley represented the most important affair in New England history. So deeply did they shake him, so manifestly did they corroborate his own sense of destiny, that he thought their outcome would determine whether America would be eternally lost or forever blessed. Thus, he said, "we must either conquer or be conquered." The work that had now begun, if it continued and prevailed, "would make New England a kind of heaven upon earth" (*Thoughts,* 384, 385). Thus, too, he felt the times demanded that he rally other ministers to the battle. Clearly the issue had little to do with whether religious conversion was or was not as tangible as Jeremiah's bowel pains. Alan Heimert says that critics erred (and still err) in exaggerating and distorting the behavior of these religiously awakened persons and "in failing to come to terms with the inward, or spiritual, qualities of the New Birth."[24] The issue concerned the terrifying reality of God in revelation. This is why in both his treatises Edwards admonished ministers never to blur the distinction between regenerate and unregenerate, between holy grace and moral suasion, and never to deceive people into believing that apart from God they could know peace. It behooved every minister to shatter such deceptions, even at the cost of terrifying his congregation with the truth.

Like certain modern Christian existentialists, Edwards believed that anxiety is a condition of the knowledge of God, just as complacency prevents this knowledge. To blame a minister for instilling anxiety among his people rather than administering comfort to them is, Edwards said, like blaming a surgeon who, despite the patient's anguish, goes on to thrust his lance further until he gets to the core of the wound. In contradistinction is the "compassionate" physician who stays his hand at the patient's first outcry, applies a bandage, leaves the core untouched, and, like New Englanders in ever growing numbers whose sense of sin had waned to near extinction, cries peace, peace, when there is no peace. Edwards called his fellow ministers to be like Christ, the disturber—or like the "wounded surgeon," as T. S. Eliot said in *Four Quartets,* who "plies the steel." They should strive to the utmost to take away fraudulent comfort from their people, even though such preaching "will terrify 'em still more" (*Thoughts,*390). Now that the Great Awakening had begun, they had to open the eyes of conscience and strike while the iron was hot. They were to disregard critics who condemned them for frightening children with talk of hell-fire. All are "heirs of hell," young or old, and "a child that has a dangerous wound may need the painful lance as well as grown persons" (*Thoughts,*394).

These are strong words. But Edwards was preaching a strong Calvinism that sought to strip illusory contentment from man. Whatever else Calvinism said about sin, one thing that Edwards insisted upon was that man's depravity had something to do with his spiritual apathy, with the fact that he was no longer disturbed by ultimate issues of existence and no longer anxious about his alienation from his real self (existing only in relation to God) and therefore his alienation from God. In this regard Edwards echoed Calvin, who, in commenting upon the passage in Jeremiah that refers to man's false security in self-glorification (9:23-24), declared that "we know God by also knowing ourselves, for these two things are bound together." And, Calvin added, "if anyone scrutinizes himself, what will he find but reason for despair?"[25]

Despite his powerful conviction that New England churches must return to vital piety, Edwards in no way sought to destroy their ecclesiastical organization as the price. Throughout his rallying cry there was also a strong note of judiciousness and strategic compromise. He realized the potency of the new wine, but he also recognized the impracticability of calling for new wine bottles. Those critics of Edwards who are wont to see him only as a flint-like Calvinist should take into account the advice he gave fellow revivalists. He cautioned them to eschew whatever appeared overly innovative—whatever "tends much to shock and surprise people's minds, and to set them a talking and disputing . . . and to swerve [them] from their great business, and turn aside to vain jangling" (*Distinguishing Marks,* 288). He called for caution and moderation. He knew too well that enough opposition already existed against such doctrines as God's absolute sovereignty, justification by faith alone, and innate depravity to wish to stir up more by indiscreet zeal. Those who view Edwards' evangelicalism as being parallel with ecclesiastical license fail to recognize his own priorities. He did not encourage uproar for the sake of piety. He understood that a fisher of men does not needlessly ruffle the water if he wishes to draw converts into his net. He knew that the strategic compromise Paul spoke of in I Corinthians 9:20-23, climaxed by the words "I am made all things to all men, that I might by all means save some," calls for expediency. Whatever other errors Edwards made, he never mistook means for ends. This straightforwardness taught him the tragic lesson that in proclaiming God's sovereignty, human means, however adroit, are never sufficient anyway.

Edwards' clarion words to his revivalist compatriots make unequivocal the only bedrock assurance on which their preaching could ever have vitality. That assurance comes when the Spirit of God has penetrated their own hearts. Much as Edwards stressed the need for diligent study, for intellectual understanding and reflection, he never veered from Calvin's insistence that the Spirit is not received "if it flits about in the top of the brain," but only when "it takes root in the depth of the heart." "I speak," said Calvin, "of nothing other than what each believer experiences within himself."[26] Reaching down to the foundations of revivalism, Edwards beckoned the clergy to search their own hearts, lest they discover as did Hawthorne's Arthur Dimmesdale that while preaching to others they are themselves castaways. Hawthorne's portrayal of this spiritual desolation in *The Scarlet Letter* takes its sombre color from Edwards' exhortation, "Oh, how miserably must such a person feel! What a wretched bondage and slavery is this! What pains, and how much art must such a minister use to conceal himself!" (*Thoughts,* 506).

No secrets of heart and mind remained hidden when Edwards, like Calvin, called for total self-scrutiny. This meant the relentless need to distinguish between true and false affections, between those affections having to do with the redeemed heart and those still darkened by nature. To clarify these distinctions was his purpose in writing *The Distinguishing Marks* and *Some Thoughts.* The same motive shaped and illumined his masterpiece, *A Treatise Concerning Religious Affections,* published in 1746. Here the polarities find brilliant definition, making the book indispensable for an understanding of Edwards' thought, including those deep windings of his inner life, so full of surging energy and feeling. In truth, whoever touches this book touches a man. *Religious Affections* brings to culmination some twenty-five years of thought about the nature of religious experience. Perry Miller has called it "the most powerful exploration of the religious psychology in all American literature."[27] It merits equal acclaim for the insight it furnishes into Edwards' own heart.

Whatever irony we find in the fact that the Awakening was finished by the time Edwards published this interpretation, or that America's intellectual direction proved him the loser to the forces represented by Charles Chauncy, or even that Edwards' work appeared alongside Benjamin Franklin's annually popular *Poor Richard's Almanac,* Edwards' great work remains indispensable for an understanding not only of eighteenth-century America but of today's religious consciousness as well. Rational scholasticism was no less bankrupt under Edwards' eye than Karl Barth saw it to be in our present century. Moreover, Edwards' radical rejection of a natural theology that assumes man capable of proving through reason the existence of God was no less massive than today's. What we have in *Religious Affections* is unmistakably polemical, to be read within the context of the waning days of America's Great Awakening. Yet it is a private work, a rich testimonial to Edwards' own sense of the heart.

4

Triumph and Tragedy

For Edwards the genuine importance of the New England revivals was what they accomplished in the hearts of men. His unflagging concern was the drama taking place deep within the consciousness of each individual. This is not to say that Edwards minimized the public effect which the revivals were having, nor is it to overlook

Edwards' interpretation of them as pieces in God's overall architecture of history. But it was always inward and downward that Edwards directed his most intense concern, even from his student days at Yale when his study of Locke posed basic epistemological problems that Edwards constantly related to the nature of the mind. As we have seen, he did not remain on the level of Locke's scientific empiricism but chose instead to probe into the core of religious life after first finding his own depths. Autobiographical things remain implicit in *Religious Affections,* consisting largely of sermons preached in 1742-1743. The overall eloquence and power of the book serve to intensify the already urgent questions he was asking of himself.

These questions pertain to two fundamental issues: the nature of religion and the distinguishing signs that follow from religious experience. Both issues presuppose the primacy of the heart. Answers and verifications come from the profound interior of human consciousness. Religion, Edwards constantly reminded his readers, is a human experience, a human response to power other than one's own. The Christian believes that through Christ this encounter with God's power is one of grace, and the effect (as "efficacious grace") upon man is a "saving" one. The emphasis Edwards brought to his interpretation of religious experience stemmed from his insistence that the core of religion is man's religious experience. All religious abstractions (theology) and truths (doctrines) must, by the fact that they are religious, involve man. For Edwards this meant man's heart, the center of his self, the integrating center of his being. Edwards called this center the will. More descriptively, he thought of it as man's affections, or inclinations. In short, the nature of religion involves the wellspring of human beingness, or what Edwards called "the affections of the soul" (*RA*,113).[28] Part I of *Religious Affections* establishes this fundamental point: religion by its nature is a religion of the heart. It follows that the redeemed heart will be inclined towards God, the unredeemed towards the dungeon of self.

What, then, are the distinguishing affections which reveal the direction of the soul? This question leads to the further one of how, when redirected by God through Christ, religious affections can be identified—how, in a word, they can be tested. It was here that the precariousness of Edwards' undertaking is to be seen. He believed not only that true religion consisted in "vigorous" and "lively" affections, but that such affections may be identified by their fruits, the "saving" signs, the chief of which was Christian practice.

In this he was drawing dangerously close to the empiricist doctrine of works which his adversaries upheld as providing authoritative basis for their notion of Christian morality, later to be called the Protestant ethic. Edwards took the risk by confronting the issue head-on. As if holding his chief insights for the last of the Twelve Signs (in Part III) of truly gracious and holy affections, he affirmed the sign of Christian practice to be "the chief of all signs of saving grace" (RA,450). All signs coalesce into Christian action that proceeds from a heart inclined towards God. Good works that arise from any other inclination are only deceptive guises that hide a heart of stone. Thus the climax of Edwards' exposition is the unity of Christian experience and practice, the inner and the outer. Integrated Christian personality receives no better description than in Edwards' words:

> Christian or holy practice is spiritual practice; and that is not the motion of a body, that knows not how, nor when, nor wherefore it moves: but spiritual practice in man, is the practice of a spirit, animating, commanding and actuating a body, to which it is united, and over which it has power given it by the Creator. And therefore the main thing in this holy practice, is the holy acts of the mind, directed and governing the motions of the body. (RA,450)

This integration brings together affections and actions: in Pauline terms, the union of what one *would do* and what one *actually does.* It also unites head and heart, will and understanding. The redeemed heart infuses the total self, including reason, imagination, language, and all manner of feeling. Thus the negative signs of religious affections (Part II) consist of those manifestations that arise from no prior religious event, no antecedent man-God encounter. One by one Edwards discounts such false signs as crying aloud ("Hosanna, Hosanna"), bodily behavior (visceral theology like dancing or feasting), verbal fluency including the easy quoting of Scripture, self-induced affections ("trips"), appearances of love, easy salvation (ethical works, philosophic idealism, cultism), and all other signs testifying not to the faith of children of light but to "the presumption of the children of darkness" (RA,176).[29] In Edwards' view these signs are negative because they are unrelated to the indwelling work of the Holy Spirit. They have no centrality in religious experience and evince no integration with the redirected heart.

What, then, are the true distinguishing signs? Edwards gives twelve, and for each he offers lengthy and penetrating exposition. We need not fully review them here, except to notice that whereas they culminate in Christian practice—in the integration of the heart and visible acts—they all originate in religious conversion. From this radical event constituting the root of Christian life grow all the subsequent fruits of the Spirit. To sever this organic and indispensable relationship was the kind of heresy widely disseminated in Edwards' day by such works as Daniel Whitby's *Discourse* (1710) and John Taylor's *The Scripture Doctrine of Original Sin Proposed to a Free and Candid Examination* (1738)—treatises that claimed to emancipate the human will from any influences of grace upon it. Accordingly, any so-called fruits were strictly those initiated by natural man, his will being free and independent by nature. It was against such outrageous heresy that Edwards' *Religious Affections* stood, along with his later *Freedom of the Will* (1754) and *Original Sin* (1758). In the 1746 treatise he did not openly declare such natural signs to be those of sin. But such is what he meant, since they spring from natural affections that necessarily come under condemnation and sin. Dedicated to identifying the ascertainable signs of true grace, the whole of *Religious Affections* rests upon the event of grace. Thus Edwards could proceed to name as holy and gracious such true signs as the love of God and neighbor, perception of moral excellence, the enlightened mind or sense of the heart, humility, quietness and mercy, a softened heart and tender spirit, a symmetry of spirit, and a spiritual appetite for attainments of the soul.

It bears repeating that Edwards believed the effects of grace to be ascertainable and visible. The Christian experience presupposed a goal to be reached, and this goal bore distinguishing signs. On the other hand, Edwards believed that the roots of this Christian practice or action could never be absolutely verified by man. No person could validate the rebirth of another; no person could be ultimately certain of his own regeneration. Only God possesses such certain knowledge. This is why even Edwards insisted that the ascertainable and visible evidences of grace can never in the end be infallible evidences. This is also why Edwards' *Religious Affections*, ostensibly about the empirical evidences of grace, is more accurately a testament about the reality of grace. His primary intention was not so much to certify religious affections as to affirm the mysterious and efficacious Spirit of God that first empowered them.

Thus the real subject of his treatise is rebirth, treated explicitly as Signs One and Seven but woven throughout the book as well. The issue concerns the chasm separating the natural man and the spiritual man, and the certainty that only to the latter come the fruits of the Spirit. The regenerate man possesses a "new spiritual sense," not a new faculty of understanding or of will but a "new foundation laid in the nature of the soul, for a new kind of exercises of the same faculty of will" (*RA*,206). The emphasis comes with the word *new:* a new kind of perception, a new spiritual sense, a new creature, a putting off the old man and a putting on the new man (*RA*,205-206, 340-341). Edwards conceived of "soul" and "direction" as inseparable if not synonymous terms. Regeneration is a matter of a redirected soul.

What again looms is the earlier question whether conversion from natural to spiritual can be this decisive and arbitrary. Is there no continuity between a natural Saul and a converted Paul, between natural affections and religious ones? Does conversion result in purity of heart, or will a residue still be present? Paul's language could be no more decisive than when in I Corinthians 15 he distinguishes between the "natural body" and the "spiritual body," the "corruption" of one and the "incorruption" of the other. Calvin fashions the same distinctions, although at times he tantalizingly draws them close together—when, for example, he writes that no man, *i.e.*, no natural man, "is without some intuition of the eternal light." Immediately he cautions the reader, however, that "this statement has to do with the common light of nature which is far inferior to faith." By such common light no man, for all his sharpness and perspicacity, can ever "penetrate to the Kingdom of God." Even at best his light remains "obscured" by sin. Unequivocally, Calvin asserts that "it is the Spirit of God alone who opens the gate of heaven to the elect."[30] The distinction between natural and special light may be no more than a hair's breadth; yet it remains an absolute distinction and therefore that of a vast gulf.

Edwards grants the same proximity. Conversion does not eradicate a certain "natural temper" in man. Even those sins to which a man by his natural constitution was inclined before his conversion may still entrap him afterward. He may fall again and again into the mire of his own and the world's "temper." Yet his nature is changed, and such a change is an abiding thing. "A swine that is of a filthy nature may be washed; but his swinish nature remains. And a dove that is of a cleanly nature may be defiled, but its cleanly nature remains" (RA, 341). Religious affections, however besmeared by the world, remain inclined towards the Spirit by which they were first converted. The distinction in Edwards' thought is no less absolute than in that of Paul and Calvin.

We have said that Edwards' ostensible purpose in *Religious Affections* was to identify the true signs of conversion. It was to this task that he devoted Part III. However, his fundamental purpose remained that of affirming the reality of conversion itself, of differentiating between the natural and the spiritual, and of testifying to the Spirit of God as Creator of all beingness. Edwards probed to deeper levels of investigation than those suggested by the empiricist criterion of "By their fruits ye shall know them." Edwards' own dictum was: By their roots ye shall know them. Unless the roots existed in God through Christ, the so-called fruits of love, humility, spiritual longing, and new perception were only deceptions and lies.

The extent to which interpreting Edwards as an empiricist leads to error and nonsense is seen in William James' assertion that *Religious Affections* is merely an elaborate working out of the empiricist criterion mentioned above. More accurately, James faults Edwards for not offering signs of conversion that are truly discernible. The fruits that Edwards attributed to a redeemed heart James finds equally present in natural man. Were it true, James argues, that a suddenly converted man is entirely different from a natural man, "there surely ought to be some exquisite class-marks, some distinctive radiance" that would identify him as radically different. Because, according to James, Edwards fails to supply convincing class-marks unique to Christian conversion and Christian practice, James dismisses Edwards as an unsuccessful empiricist whose data lacks sufficient verifiability. As for the conversion experience itself, James finds such "roots . . . inaccessible" to empirical investigation.[31] As for the awakened heart that Edwards described, James asserts that there is "not one decisive trait, not one mark, that unmistakably parts it off from what may possibly be only an exceptionally high degree of natural goodness." "In fact," James continues, "one could hardly read a clearer argument than this book [*Religious Affections*] unwittingly offers in favor of the thesis that no chasm exists between the order of human excellence, but that here as elsewhere, nature shows continuous difference, and generation and regeneration are matters of degree."[32]

But when James acknowledged that the roots of religious affections were "inaccessible" to his investigation, he unwittingly negated his own case against Edwards. He severed the relationship signified in Edwards' criterion that presupposed roots before fruits. Failing to follow Edwards to the level of religious conversion, where according to Christian orthodoxy the roots of existence receive new life, James understandably rejected the essential distinction Edwards made between nature and grace. What becomes equally clear is that James, limited by his self-restricting methods, failed to see that Edwards' *Religious Affections* was written within the circle of religious faith. James' observations made from outside this context inevitably went awry when he claimed them as authoritative about matters within it. Instead of looking with Edwards, James looked at him. Comparison between the two stances resembles that which Kierkegaard described as between the natural man and the Christian; it was like "the relation between a child and a man. . . . The child does not know what the dreadful is; this the man knows and he shudders at it."[33] The one's perception is not the other's; neither is the natural man's the Christian's. The causal roots in perception make all the difference. To have experienced this difference as a participant and not as a spectator, to have recognized it to be one of radical and saving change and not as mere accretive knowledge, was the essence of Edwards' triumph.

To say this draws one immediately back to Edwards' concept of the sense of the heart and to its essential privacy. Throughout his treatise a haunting undertone reminds us that in the end there are no visible and infallible evidences of religious affections. No one can see into another's heart to determine its inclinations; "much of it is in secret, and hid from the eye of the world" (*RA,* 420). The fact that much of it also is hidden from oneself accounts in part for the shudder that Kierkegaard's Christian knows so well. The point is pivotal in our discussion of Edwards because insofar as his "triumph" occurred in the private heart, it was in the public pulpit that his tragedy took place. It was there Edwards insisted that such privacy be made public through professed testimony. Had he said that the true fruits of the Spirit—love, peace, joy, humility, insight, practice—defy distinguishing marks, he would have bespoken their true mystery. He also would have been content, if such is the term, to have allowed the Great Awakening to do its own mysterious work in the private hearts of his congregation.

But as James Carse points out in his study of Edwards' search for a visible faith, Edwards expected something more radically revolutionary than private conversion. He expected the redeemed to profess their faith. In 1742 he drew up a covenant for his congregation to sign, binding the signers to live their faith visibly—to love their neighbors, to do nothing through tongue or commercial profiteering to injure them, to give daily evidence of their spiritual experience. Two years later he demanded verbal profession of faith as the necessary qualification for one's partaking of the Lord's Supper. According to Carse, what Edwards finally expected was the church to be a community of professing, visible saints who accepted their responsibility as leaders "in the long journey toward the ultimate society."[34] When the members, in turn, realized that Edwards was in earnest about this vision, when they suspected that he was reshaping the church from its previous role of service to that of Edwards' rule, when they found that their shorter vision of moral sincerity was being contravened by his longer one of saving holiness, they did to him what the Genevans had done to Calvin. By a vote of 230 to 23, the Northampton congregation ratified the Council's recommendations to dismiss him.

The whole affair has its nontheological antecedents, most of them unpleasant. In 1744 there was the so-called "bad book" incident involving some understandably inquisitive children who somehow had come into possession of a handbook for midwives. Thinking such reading unsuitable for young minds, Edwards retained his congregation one morning so that they might hear the names of the culprits. But in reading from his list he failed to distinguish between the apparent offenders and the mere supernumeraries. Parents were outraged by Edwards' tactlessness. Other incidents concerned what some townspeople thought to be the material extravagance of the Edwards family. The Edwards' family budget was subjected to regular public scrutiny, and Edwards had to wait until 1747 before his request for a fixed salary was granted. The town gossipers never lacked topics.

In his account of Edwards' last half dozen years in Northampton Perry Miller weaves together the details of the "bad book" fiasco and of the unpopular measures Edwards devised for creating visibility among his saints. Miller's tapestry contains astonishing language. Edwards "bullied" his congregation into drawing up the 1742 oath. He was "proud," "overbearing," "rash"; he practiced "concealment" until it became "second nature"; his "arrogance" was symptomatic of "a more profound dislocation." "Was he stupid?" "Was he arrogant?," Miller asks when recounting Edwards' recital of the children's names. That Edwards displayed "fantastic insensibility" Miller has no doubt. Neither does Miller question Edwards' "ruthless diplomacy," befitting a "fiendish torturer of writhing spiders" whose destructive passion all along, according to Miller's slippery handling of Freud, was aimed not at his father, Timothy Edwards, but at the redoubtable ghost of his grandfather, Solomon Stoddard. Little wonder, Miller goes on, that "nowhere else did the mass of a town hate a man as the citizenry of Northampton hated Edwards." Edwards' insistence that members profess their faith before taking communion was, to Miller, a "long-delayed disclosure of his deviation from Stoddard," "a criminal tergiversation, a masterpiece of treason to the community." Little wonder that Edwards "was cursed from one end of the Valley to the other."[35]

Such details do not make the fabric of tragedy. Were they as Miller describes them, the Northampton controversy would have been little more than the melodrama of angry citizens dangling their minister over the town fires of rebuke. What does emerge from the controversy is the tragedy of a man whose singular vision was smashed by those persons who refused to perform their part in it. In his tragedy he envisioned too boldly and expected too much. He made the desperate wager that the reality and the profession of it might be one and the same. It was a wager that held majestic possibilities. After "long searching, pondering, viewing, and reviewing," he took his stand. What was at stake, he said, was "my own reputation, future usefulness, and my very subsistence" (*Humble Inquiry*, I, 432). This was the price Northampton exacted. Edwards paid it. But unlike Calvin, he never enjoyed the vindication of being asked to return.

Suspecting the outcome but hoping to forestall it, Edwards resolutely set to work in the summer of 1749 to defend his position in a substantial treatise entitled *An Humble Inquiry into the Rules of the Word of God, Concerning the Qualifications Requisite to a Complete Standing and Full Communion in the Visible Christian Church*. He hoped that his opponents would read his carefully drawn statement, so that even if they dismissed him they at least would be able first to meet him upon common intellectual ground.

The *Humble Inquiry* is a brilliant *tour de force* setting forth the doctrines of conversion, profession, and communion. In this same order was to be seen the rite of Christian visibility. Edwards once again insisted that conversion is of the heart, where one either loves God or hates him. He granted no other options. Because conversion comes through grace, the Christian's duty is to "own" the Covenant of Grace publicly, to profess the consent of his heart to it. It is not enough that he understand the Covenant or even that he understand his obligation to comply with it; only as he professes the consent and compliance of his heart can he be said to own it. He first brings his heart to the Covenant ("He that keeps back his heart, does in effect keep back all"—I, 444), then he professes in words the spiritual experience. The word becomes sacramental; it is "nigh thee," said Paul, "even in thy mouth, and in thy heart" (Romans 10:8). Edwards strove to unite the heart and the word. In this, he said, is "the sum and substance of true piety" (I, 443). Without the heart, the word is hollow. Contrariwise, without the word, the heart remains invisible.

Communion is a further outward sign—"A visible form of invisible grace," Augustine had said—that seals the Covenant. Like a marriage, the Covenant requires two consenting parties: Christ's part is salvation, the Christian's part is faith. Communion, then, is "a mutual solemn profession of the two parties transacting the covenant of grace, and visibly united in that covenant" (I,458). Through the sacramental bread and wine

> Christ presents himself to the believing communicants . . . and they, in receiving what is offered, and eating and drinking the symbols of Christ's body and blood, also profess their part in the covenant of grace. . . . Indeed what is professed on both sides is the *heart:* for Christ, in offering himself, professes the willingness of his heart to be theirs who truly receive him; and the communicants, on their part, profess the willingness of their hearts to receive him, which they declare by *significant actions* [*i.e.*, verbal profession of faith]. (I,459, italics mine)

Edwards meant "significant actions" to be words, professing words. He considered them as important to communion as the bread and wine representing Christ's visible presence. Heart-words represented the communicant's visible heart at the Table. The "established signs" of bread and wine "are fully equivalent to words" (I,459).

It was a supremely bold position to take. Was he asking for the impossible? He had carefully followed Calvin's doctrine of the sacraments, especially the crucial point concerning faith as the prerequisite for every communicant. Like Calvin he had further said that conversion does not depend upon the sacraments. To both thinkers the notion that sacraments justify man and confer grace was absurd, worthy of medieval scholastics and, Edwards might have added, eighteenth-century Arminians.[36] Justification comes only through faith, and grace only through Christ. But Edwards also argued for *professed* faith, faith made verbal through the only sacramental offering man can bring, namely, words. The implications of what Edwards required were terrifying.

Each person before taking the bread and wine must examine himself; either profess his worthiness or confess his unworthiness; and then, if he partook of the elements, live with the tormenting doubt that he had partaken unworthily and thereby, as Paul warned, had eaten and drunk "damnation to himself" (I Cor. 11:29). Because verbal profession added another dimension to communion, the communicant became that much more vulnerable to falsehood and deception.

In Edwards' reasoning a slight fissure opened ominously between stage two (profession) and stage three (communion). This is what proved his undoing, inevitable for anyone who seeks to pass judgment upon the integrity of another. Woe to the preacher, Melville's Father Mapple might have said, who imposes his own conscience upon that of another; who dares to determine the spirit behind another's word; who seeks to authenticate what can only be self-authenticating. Something in these admonishments dimly suggests what Hawthorne called the "sanctity" of another's heart. Woe to the preacher who violates it.

Edwards knew the danger. Yet Edwards believed that as the appointed and ordained minister, as a public official of the church, it was his duty to be the visible "eye of the church's Christian judgment" (I,435). The applicant stands in *foro ecclesiae*, before the church, in Christian judgment; the minister stands as the eye of "reason sanctified, regulated, and enlightened, by a principle of Christian love" (I,437). Whatever Edwards expected of others, what he expected of himself left no question: it was purity of heart made visible in the purity of his judgment upon others. Even though one dare not write "hubris" across Edwards' portrait, nemesis seems strangely to have been at work. Those whom Edwards judged became his own judges. In his "Farewell Sermon" he chose the theme of judgment—theirs upon him, his upon them, and, finally, in a dimension that reaches beyond tragedy, God's judgment upon all.

CHAPTER THREE

Imagination and Vision

1
Imagination and Epistemology

Edwards' theology rests upon an epistemological foundation: what we know depends upon how we know. We have examined Edwards' misgivings about knowledge which is derived from mere cognition. Such knowledge, which Edwards called notional and speculative, never satisfactorily answered the great religious questions about sin, alienation, faith, grace, and holiness. Such knowledge may enhance understanding; yet understanding derived from intellectual speculation never opened the deeper levels of consciousness where Edwards did his theological work. An alternative was sensible knowledge, knowledge that springs from feelings and somehow engages a greater portion of human personality. This knowledge creates within the mind a sense of things, an intuited conviction, a sight that transforms abstract truth into "actual ideas" inseparable from feelings. [1] Without sensible knowledge a person lacks this fuller dimension of truth; he remains outside, detached, separated. Edwards believed that in religious matters we dare not disregard sensible knowledge.

This division between thought and feeling—hardly as arbitrary as I have suggested here, yet fundamental in Edwards' epistemology [2] — breaks into yet another division: nature and spirit. Thought is both natural and sanctified; likewise, feelings are those that all natural men experience and those that only the regenerate know. Going either the way of thought or the way of feeling, one inevitably arrives at this other distinction separating the thoughts and feelings of natural man from those of the regenerate man. This distinction is arbitrary; it is ordained by God through Christ and is the basis of Christian knowledge. Regardless of how far one goes with speculative knowledge, or how much farther with sensible knowledge, the way stops at that point where this distinction between nature and spirit becomes real.

For example, sensible knowledge common to natural man includes aesthetics and imagination. From such knowledge comes a certain awakening that mere thinking cannot produce. The awakened mind is sensible to natural beauty, to sounds and sights, to appetites, even to something Edwards regarded as natural good and evil. Sensible knowledge, surpassing "a mere notion," may even bring to natural man a sense of "God's greatness, power and awful majesty," as well as a sense of human finitude and guilt.[3] Through his active natural capacities, a person can apprehend a great deal about himself and God. But after all this is granted, there still remains the stumbling block: natural man has a "natural stupidity of the soul," and without divine assistance he can never have sensible knowledge of those things of religion most profound and most glorious. For all his convictions about natural beauty, human vision, and God's wrath as well as blessedness, he still lacks the sensible apprehension of the *spiritual* excellency of divine things. Without this he has no "SPIRITUAL CONVICTION of the truth of divine things"; he has no "SAVING FAITH [*sic*]."[4] It is here where the distinguishing essence is to be found. Only through spirit as distinct from nature does a sense of the divine excellency of the things of religion become real.

This saving spirit is the gift of God. As Douglas J. Elwood puts it, "God initiates the life of the Spirit in man by communicating Himself in terms of an 'immediate light.' "[5] Only after God initiates this light of grace can man intuit God's highest attributes, namely, excellency and beauty. The illumination is neither common nor natural but spiritual—the special, saving, infusing, revealing work of God. According to Edwards, what we know about Christian truth depends upon how we know. This is to say that such knowledge is obtained only in a state of grace. Therefore, underlying all such knowledge is the event, the saving man-God event through Christ. This event takes place in the heart, in the ravished and transformed heart, in the very core of human beingness, including man's reason and his consenting mind. Thus the redeemed heart is at once the "whatness" and the "howness" of Christian knowledge. Such knowledge constitutes the Christian's new foundation of being. All subsequent knowledge bears upon the experience of conversion. In short, what we know depends finally upon what we are. The Christian knows because the light in which he lives is the light that nature (darkness) neither comprehends nor extinguishes.

The mystery of the epistemological event defies analysis. This is why Edwards, even though he tried to make careful distinctions, also saw these same distinctions mysteriously fuse together. For example, the sense of the heart is also instructional. The sense affects cognition. As Edwards repeatedly said, one who perceives the sweet taste of honey knows more about it cognitively than one who only looks at honey (II,14; RA,272).[6] His cognition is affected by his identity. Redemptive experience integrates understanding and will, and ultimately makes discrete distinctions irrelevant. Furthermore, Edwards saw that sensible knowledge that is natural fuses with sensible knowledge that is spiritual. The former, as we have said, stops short of the spiritual knowledge of God's divine excellency that Edwards reserved for the regenerate. Yet the prerequisite for this latter knowledge is not only divine assistance or grace, clearly beyond nature, but also active natural sensation, an active mind fully sensible to the finite world in all its beauty and corruption. A saving sense of God's excellency depends "in some measure and more indirectly and remotely" upon the sensible apprehension of what is natural.[7]

This is an important point. For Edwards, even while distinguishing between the natural and the spiritual, again recognizes in the event of conversion a mystery that issues forth in paradox: man does all, God does all. While stressing God's divine initiative, Edwards also calls for the total activity of natural understanding and will. His is neither the Romantic's call to fall asleep in body and become a living soul nor the Gnostic's pure, elite spirituality. Instead Edwards summons all the mean capacities in man, all that is finite and limited. Only then does the man-God paradox become dynamic; the Christian's way down also becomes his way up, and the way into natural things the perfect separation from them.[8]

All these matters, though prefatory, are significant when we consider imagination in Edwards' epistemology. We recall that imagination belongs to the domain of sensible rather than speculative knowledge. As such it is distinct from reason and the ways of science. In his early essay "Of the Prejudices of Imagination," inserted into Notes on "The Mind," Edwards denounced the rationalists ("the Learned world") who had supposedly "conquered" imagination. He was emboldened to suggest that the reason many learned (but unnamed) rationalists still preferred Ptolemy was that they could not tolerate what their imagination conceived as a vaster universe. Edwards here is referring to natural imagination or to what Professor Howard calls the "philosophical or unregenerate imagination," the endowment of natural man. What we are concerned with is the "regenerate imagination" (again Howard's term) that owes its quality to the sense of the heart, the event of conversion.[9] Both kinds of imagination recall the dichotomy between natural and spiritual. To follow where the dichotomy leads, to examine Edwards' ideas about imagination and to step afoot with his vision, takes us into the center of Edwards' theological world.

2
Natural Imagination

In his total writings the importance Edwards gave to the subject of imagination does not readily appear. To the eighteenth-century mind the subject was hardly the most urgent. Any importance it claimed among theologians, especially those molded by Puritan dialectic, was largely negative. The reason was simple enough. Among all man's natural capacities, the imagination was the most susceptible to the devil's wiles. With due seriousness Edwards heeded such warnings. In *Religious Affections* he quotes the English Puritan, Anthony Burgess: " 'The imagination is that room of the soul, wherein the devil doth often appear.' " The reference is to the unregenerate imagination destitute of grace, the imagination from which, according to Burgess, "horrible" and "diabolical" delusions arise (*RA*,289n). Edwards did not need to go beyond his own Connecticut Valley for verification. After all, it was the horrendous imaginings of the Enthusiasts that Edwards excluded from the legitimate and distinguishing marks of Christian experience. Yet he recognized a strange power in such imaginings. Dangerous as they were, how blessed they might become once the heart had been redeemed! No measurement could describe the reaches the regenerate imagination might attain.

Even while revivals thundered and all manner of presentiments flashed before New England congregations, Edwards cautiously acknowledged human nature to be such that "we cannot think of things invisible, without a degree of imagination." The more engaged the mind and intense the affections (Edwards' stellar objectives), the "still more lively and strong will the imaginary idea ordinarily be" (*Distinguishing Marks*, 236). To experience the "imaginary idea" as the actual idea, like fear or joy, is to know the idea as event. Here Edwards is not necessarily referring to imagination touched by grace. His concern is with imagination *per se* that bridges speculative and sensible knowledge, unifies the poles of reason and sensation, and thereby embraces the totality of natural existence. Imagination mediates between intellect and sense. The extent to which Edwards' own imagination unified these two spheres led Perry Miller to call him a "theologian of mediation," the first in American history to weave together "pure understanding, which was reason and [Charles] Chauncy, and the mystery, which was terror and the spider."[10] The mediating imagination is also somehow prophetic; it is prophetic because it is creative; it is creative because the new synthesis it creates perpetually stretches out to include reality heretofore unattainable—the past, the future, the invisible. Imagination mediates between appearance and ultimate truth, claims kinship with everything, and brings the real into being. To say, as Edwards does, that we need imagination in order to know the invisible and spiritual is also to say, on the strictly humanistic level, that we need it to save us from skepticism, ignorance, and barbarity.[11]

There is something intoxicating about the idea of human imagination that mediates between the extreme reaches of the mind, extending experience to an imaginative hell and to an imaginative heaven. The renowned myth critic Northrop Frye suggests that our world is as large as imagination makes it. By means of such promethean power, the poet takes us to the depths and heights, corresponding to the conceptions of hell and heaven and their equivalent myths. What the poet writes, Frye says, is "a human apocalypse, man's revelation to man." Nothing is outside the imagination because it has "swallowed" everything, even time and space.[12] What beguiling possibilities does natural imagination thus possess! Should existence ever appear so absurd as to overwhelm us with nausea, the "sorceress expert in healing"—Nietzsche's term for art—can turn our "fits of nausea into imaginations with which it is possible to live." So powerful to Nietzsche is the artist's imaginative energy that art becomes redemptive in the "transcendent serenity" and the "metaphysical solace" it provides. Nietzsche believed that only as we awaken to "the Dionysiac bird"—the dove, the holy spirit, the redemptive power of human imagination—can we ever "staunch the eternal wound of being." Such awakening occurs when we come before Nietzsche's trinity: Bach, Beethoven, and Wagner.[13]

Of course Edwards would have damned such unbridled imagining and the pride from which it springs. Even if so-called natural imagination be articulated as human apocalypse, the human dimension is necessarily a limited one. Edwards never mitigated the truth of this fact. Although his own artistry rose to compelling intensity, awakening the imagination of those persons still decidedly numbered among the unregenerate; although his sermons crackled with the behest, "Imagine . . . Imagine . . . " ("The Future Punishment. . . ," II,81); although his explosions of imagery scarcely left the audience any choice but to comply, natural imagination having indeed sufficed to bring to life both terror and tranquility; yet Edwards never considered it the way to spiritual discoveries. Those persons who did suffered outrageous delusions. In spite of the expansiveness that human imagination commanded, the vision that was forthcoming was by definition limited and corrupted. To suppose that imaginative art provided metaphysical solace and redemption doubly verified the delusions.

What troubled Edwards during the Great Awakening was not only the legalistic hypocrisy he saw among the Arminians but also the evangelistic hypocrisy among persons who were carried away by impulse and imagined revelations (RA, 173-174). Thus he deemed it necessary to warn against imagination when he saw it counterfeiting true spiritual light. Constantly distinguishing between what he considered the true and the false in religious matters, Edwards warned that natural imagination is never more than a "common gift" that all men possess (Thoughts, 436). Natural imaginings must not be mistaken for those inspired by divine agency. When Enthusiasts heard "voices" and beheld "visions," claimed that such revelations came from God, and then based their religious affections upon these experiences, Edwards knew the issue demanded stern clarification:

> Thus when the Spirit of God gives a natural man visions, as he did Balaam, he only impresses a natural principle, viz. the sense of seeing, immediately exciting ideas of that sense; but he gives no new sense; neither is there anything supernatural, spiritual or divine in it. So if the Spirit of God impresses on a man's imagination, either in a dream, or when he is awake, any outward ideas of any of the senses, either voices, or shapes and colors, 'tis only exciting ideas of the same kind that he has by natural principles and senses. (*RA*,206-207)

A man may have thousands of such revelations. His imagination may create varieties of religious experience that include the most sublime aesthetic moments. Yet to regard such experience as evidence of religious affection when the heart is devoid of grace is to be guilty of evangelistic pretense.

It was never Edwards' purpose to denigrate imagination and the aesthetic vision. On the contrary, he conceived of theological issues in aesthetic terms, beauty being an ontological model. Roland André Delattre has argued that Edwards, unlike Calvin, conceived of God in terms of beauty, not power. Although to both theologians divine majesty was supremely important, for Calvin it was an "awful and awesome" majesty replete with terror and darkness, whereas for Edwards it radiated beauty and light.[14] The point is that unaided natural imagination is never adequate to this conception of beauty. This is the real substance of Edwards' admonishment. Imagination untouched by grace yields no spiritual discoveries, it gives no new sense. It may enable natural man to have tentative conceptions about spiritual affections, but of the nucleus or kernel he has no more conception than one born blind has of colors. Adamant about these ultimate distinctions, Edwards averred that in matters pertaining to religious truth the spiritually destitute imagination leaves a person no better than "totally blind, deaf and senseless, yea dead" (*RA*,274).

The danger occurs when one thinks otherwise, when the treachery of the devil obscures the crucial distinction between "lively imaginations arising from strong [religious] affections, and strong affections arising from lively imaginations" (*RA*,291). The first is the way of blessedness and vision; the second, the byway to Satan's precincts of pride and delusion. In the end Edwards' warning is profoundly simple: natural imagination embraces nothing unless the soul through faith first embraces God. Only then is the imagination sanctified; and for this, the redeemed heart is the *conditio sine qua non.*

The term "embrace" is Edwards' metaphor. Its meaning is radically different from what Northrop Frye suggests when he heralds the "educated" imagination as that which has "swallowed" all time and space, all depths and heights, and then has issued forth as "a human apocalypse." As H. Richard Niebuhr reminds us, this kind of imagination is characterized by egotism.[15] All the world is centered in the "I." Waging a kind of counter-Copernican revolution, the imagination establishes the universe as egocentric and all truth as solipsism. In contrast, the sanctified imagination presupposes a consenting soul. In this connection Edwards used the word "embrace." By it he meant the act of one's believing, the soul's "entirely embracing . . . entirely adhering and acquiescing" in Christian revelation.[16] Only as the soul embraces or consents to the perfect excellency of God as revealed in Christ will the imagination discover "the beauty of the Godhead, and the divinity of Divinity . . . the good of the infinite Fountain of Good" (*RA,*274). A person imagines nothing who does not imagine this. Underlying the equation is Edwards' dictum: man believes that he might truly imagine. Whereas natural imagination makes man the center, sanctified imagination embraces all things and thus enables him to hope all things and to endure all things. When in man, the center cannot hold; when in God, it orders all things and through Christ unfolds them to our new sight.

3
Sanctified Imagination

To speculate about the new sight that comes through grace raises important questions about the nature of religious imagination. To what extent can such imagination surpass the limitations of speculative reason and natural imagination? Furthermore, to what extent is it necessary to deny empirical knowledge to make room for religious faith?[17] In what way does faith enable one to see more clearly even though the glass of vision is never perfect? Does religious imagination through faith answer questions about the meaning of man, his destiny, his highest goal, more satisfactorily than philosophic thought? What is to prevent any individual from claiming such powers of sight and then acting capriciously upon them? How does one distinguish between Abraham and Herman Melville's Ahab, Dante's pilgrim and Ibsen's Brand, St. John of *Revelation* and William Golding's Jocelin in *The Spire* (1964), Kierkegaard's knight of faith and Goethe's Faust—all claiming to have been graced with power beyond nature and to have been given what Edwards called "a new spiritual sense"? In short, what basis of truth can religious imagination claim when such truth patently cannot be verified and when its dangers are those of damnation itself?

In answering such problems, Edwards returned again and again to special grace as differentiated from common grace (and natural imagination) that merely assists the faculties in doing more fully what they already do by nature. Special grace "causes the faculties to do that which they do not by nature and of which there is nothing of the like kind in the soul by nature."[18] The gift of special grace is the sanctified imagination. Not only does the regenerate receive a new foundation and inclination of will but he possesses a new imaginative power by which to apprehend what before was invisible. Edwards called these apprehensions "illuminations," the foremost being those of beauty and glory. Essential in Edwards' thought is the fact that God is the "author" of the new capacity to see. We see God's glory when the new sense of the heart includes us in this glory. Imagination embraces it because we stand within its circle.

Although Edwards' basis for religious imagination is singularly theological, one should not suppose that theology was only theoretical and logical to Edwards. When citing special grace as the underlying answer to questions about imagination, he did not mean that these questions suddenly lost their mystery. Edwards never intended theology to simplify matters, nor did he think theology simple. Theology carried the same risks as did life because Edwards knit both together according to decisions of belief that defied logical verification. That through grace religious imagination makes possible spiritual illuminations beyond normal experience was for Edwards a faith that demanded the commitment of his total self. It was this very totality that was at stake in the decisions of belief. A theological answer was a religious one that affirmed not only the mystery but also the spiritual sense that perceives it.

"Imagination," says Richard Kroner, "can perform its religious function only when man from whom imagination springs is included in the divine mystery, or, more precisely, when it is this mystery itself that works in man."[19] This mysterious force customarily termed inspiration implies a power at work within man but greater than his own creative energy. It engenders religious imagination which, as Kroner says, bridges the "gap" between man and the divine mystery. We can say that religious imagination, no less mysterious than its content or product, is inspiration from the side of man and divine revelation from the side of God. Through imagination sanctified by God's Spirit the saint sees everything as related to divine mystery. As Kroner points out, the world no longer exists merely for man's practical use, theoretical contemplation, or aesthetic intuition.[20] The saint sees the world stamped as part of divine creation and subject to God's intervening wrath and love. He sees everything in the world as images or shadows of divine things. The world is not only symbolical but sacramental in the sense that the regenerate eye beholds it as existing within the unity of divine meaning. It is this sacramental dimension that is visible only to the sanctified imagination, for there is no sacramental object apart from the special heartfelt sense that grasps it.

When Edwards wrote of the sanctified ear and eye, he meant the new spiritual sense that God graciously gives, enabling man to perceive this miraculous element in all phenomena (*Thoughts*,436-437). Seen by the regenerate eye, nature is full of divine emanations. Edwards thought of these as images embodying ontological truth. The distinction between rhetorical and ontological images, or between "tropes" and "types," we find carefully explained in Perry Miller's introduction to Edwards' *Images or Shadows of Divine Things*, a private notebook of some 212 entries that saw the light of publication in 1948, nearly two hundred years after Edwards died.[21] To Edwards rivers, trees, mountains, birds, the sun, the moon were not to be considered mere rhetorical tropes, common in the richly ornamented prose of the seventeenth-century Anglican divines, but rather to be held as "types" that imaged or shadowed forth their spiritual "antitypes." Nature is still nature, mutable and corrupt; yet its essence, Edwards believed, is not in mutability or corruption but in the spiritual reality of which the sun and rivers and trees are the images.

> The sun's so perpetually, for so many ages, sending forth his rays in such vast profusion, without any diminution of his light and heat, is a bright image of the all-sufficiency and everlastingness of God's bounty and goodness.
>
> * * * *
>
> And so likewise are the rivers, which are ever flowing, that empty vast quantities of water every day and yet there is never the less to come. The spirit communicated and shed abroad, that is to say, the goodness of God, is in Scripture compared to a river and the trees that grow and flourish by the river's side through the benefit of the water represent the saints who live upon Christ and flourish through the influences of his spirit.
>
> * * * *
>
> The silk-worm is a remarkable type of Christ. Its greatest work is weaving something for our beautiful clothing, and it dies in this work; it spends its life on it, it finishes it in death (as Christ was obedient unto death, his righteousness was chiefly wrought but in dying), and then it rises again, a worm as Christ was in his state of humiliation, but a more glorious creature when it rises. . . .
>
> * * * *
>
> When the fruit is ripe, it is easily gathered; it does not cleave fast to the tree, but is ready to quit it, and is picked without rending or making any wound. So is a saint that is ripe for heaven, he easily quits this world.[22]

True spiritual sense discovers coherence in universal being, a divine agency in the world of historical and daily events, a divinity that shapes our ends. Everything becomes miraculous as the invisible enters the common world of trees and stones and the unknown appears under historical circumstances. What other human faculty, Edwards asked, can decipher history and grasp the interpenetration of the divine and the human but sanctified imagination? How else does the believer experience God's revelation—"the glory of God's works, both of creation and providence" (RA,273)? With a true sense of the spirit, the regenerate "will view nothing as he did before" (RA,275). Just as there is such a thing as "good taste of natural beauty . . . there is likewise such a thing as divine taste" in discerning spiritual emanations (RA,282-283).

Edwards conceived of imagination as having more to do with discovery than with creativity. Reality already exists, to be discovered by a graceful imagination, an inspired *intuitus*.[23] In the later Coleridgean view, imagination shapes a wholly new reality out of the elements first assimilated into its organic processes. This view allows the poet to create a new poetic image. But Edwards would have insisted that because the poet's image was first taken from the visible world which he did not create, true creation belongs to God and the real image already embodies divine truth. In other words, divine creation precedes human creativity. All questions about what humans create are subsumed into divine creation, and aesthetic forms have importance only in relation to metaphysical reality. When, therefore, Edwards speaks of a new sense that goes beyond natural imagination, he is not referring to what Coleridge in the nineteenth century called the secondary imagination, that capacity to create something new out of what the primary imagination first collected and sorted out.[24] Edwards thought of the religious imagination as the capacity to discover what already exists and, in the end, to apprehend the full beauty and glory of the Creator. Although, as we shall notice later, Edwards stressed the importance of language, he believed the imaginative force behind words to be more a discerning than a shaping one.

It is unfortunate that Edwards wrote comparatively little on the subject of imagination. Yet it is also open to us to observe Edwards' own imagination at work, how it brought forth dazzling illuminations that seemed to eventuate in unstoppable words. Miller thinks that *Images or Shadows of Divine Things* provides such an example, revealing "successive moments of illumination" that terminated in "ecstatic cry when the words were thrown on the paper in exclamation that defies the restraints of prose."[25] For all their power, the greater power is what lies beneath his words. This we may properly call the discerning power of his imagination. It is the implicit theme of the *Images* and the impelling force behind his sermons.

In order to discern the full sacramental dimension of the world, Edwards presupposed an imagination rooted in the power of the heart. It is in the prior experience of the redeemed heart that Edwards believed all the sources of imagination come together, and the first obligation of anyone who claims to envision the wonder of the invisible world is to affirm this original integration, the gift of grace. Jacques Maritain gives a remarkable account of the process.

This total integrity Maritain calls "repose," the sense that comes to
the soul when it is in "spiritual contact" with itself. It is, he says, a
state of "refreshment and peace superior to any feeling." The human
soul dies but to live again "in exaltation and enthusiasm." The
invigorated and vivified mind

> enters a happy activity, so easy that everything seems to be given it at
> once, and, as it were, from the outside. In reality everything was there,
> kept in the shade, hidden in the spirit and in the blood; all that which will
> be manifested in operation was already there, but we knew it not. We knew
> neither how to discover nor how to use it, before having gained new forces
> in those tranquil depths.[26]

Maritain makes clear that the "enthusiasm" arising from the
tranquil center of the soul has nothing to do with delirium and
frenzy, which, he explains, are only tokens of the weakness of
nature and proceed from spurious sources. Spirit does not work this
way. The "real blessing" is poetic intuition, not any kind of thrill.[27]
Even though at this point Maritain is not writing explicitly from
within the context of Christian theology, and thus does not specify
the redeemed heart as the real blessing, he nevertheless regards the
gift of intuition as the most "spiritual" and "catalytic" agent of
inspiration, and suggests that inspiration and the divine grace that
fortifies it work together.

This account helps us to understand the basis upon which Edwards finally rejected the Enthusiasts of the New England revivals.
Their imaginings were neither founded upon the real blessing of
grace nor integrated with the redeemed heart. Thus their visions
beheld nothing of divine illumination.

In all these matters Edwards is first and last a Christian theologian. However much his theory of "types" resembles Ralph Waldo
Emerson's later view that all natural things are emblematic of spiritual things;[28] however close his ideas about spiritual sense seem to
those of the Antinomians and Quakers; and however tempted one
may be to subtly transform Edwards' ideas on imagination into a
theory of creativity, an all-important claim quickly dispels coinci-
dental similarities. That one claim has to do with Christ as the final
and ultimate mediator between human imagination and divine truth.
Only through Christ can one know the beauty of divine creation and
providence. Only this way can he truly see river, tree, and sun as

"types." Edwards punctured any illusion suggesting that human imagination circumvents the fact of Christ. For unless Christ is seen first, "nothing is seen, that is worth seeing: for there is no other true excellency or beauty" (*RA,274*). Only by this *a priori* condition can we know anything more "than the devils do" (*RA,273*). Reflecting the singlemindedness of Paul and anticipating that of Karl Barth, Edwards insisted that Christian sight comes only through the special impact which the Creator through Christ makes upon us. To question or reject this special revelation is to stand condemned, as if one's body were to reject one's heart.

Only as imagination functions within Christian revelation does Edwards regard it as creative; only as it first discerns and then responds to the Creator can it be said to envision creatively. What Edwards wanted completely clear is the distinction between Creator and creature. He never denied the importance of an active imagination. But its true activity originates in response to God who is the origin of all creative activity. Therefore, only as human imagination (the "I") envisions and creates from within the context of Christian revelation (the "Thou") can it be trusted. Outside this context it is self-initiating, self-creating, and, therefore, by definition, arrogant, proud, sinful. Its visions and creations are only delusions of grandeur.

We must remember that Edwards grounded his ideas in a Calvinist system containing certain propositions about the nature of man and God. The chief one is God's sovereignty and man's dependence. To sin is to reverse this relationship and to make man including his imagination independent of God. Calvin's perspective helps us to see the difference between, for example, a Jean-Jacques Rousseau and an Augustine, both of whom wrote separate *Confessions* that included investigations into their respective sources of creative power. For Rousseau temperament was a kind of absolute. In an ontological sense, his feelings and experiences were his alone. For Augustine such self-containment proved a curse. Only as his feelings were in response to a greater reality could he acknowledge them as sources for creative vision. Though they were his, they originated from another source and lived only within that infinitely greater dimension. The issue, we see, concerns the difference between the non-Christian and the Christian imagination, between the unbelieving and the Christian creative person. Admittedly we have structured a risky dichotomy. Both persons may be equally innovative in turning away from the past and creating something new from sources unique to their own experiences. Furthermore, the unbeliever may surpass the Christian in terms of whatever aesthetic criteria we use. But there is a difference, says C. S. Lewis:

> The unbeliever may take his own temperament and experience, just as they happen to stand, and consider them worth communicating simply because they are facts or, worse still, because they are his. To the Christian his own temperament and experience, as mere fact, and as merely his, are of no value or importance whatsoever: he will deal with them, if at all, only because they are the medium through which, or the position from which, something universally profitable appeared to him.[29]

We see more clearly the difference between an imagination that "swallows" (Frye's term) all things into itself and one that "embraces" (Edwards' term) all things through faith. The difference is finally between (1) man as the independent repository of truth, the more subjective the more valid, and (2) man whose very identity consists in his relationship with the Creator. Taken all the way, the former position ends with man's humanity corroborated by his alienation. In this alienated (independent) state he shapes his values, imagines his glory, and constructs his tower of Babel. The latter position establishes man's humanity at that moment when he recognizes the impact of God upon him. To this revelation he resigns himself, in it he loses himself to his own greater glory, and his apotheosis is the vision of a new city of God not rising from the plains but descending from the heavens. In embracing this reality, sanctified imagination expands infinitely farther than does natural imagination, which in swallowing the *mysterium tremendum* transforms it into human dross.

4

Vision

One is tempted to think of such terms as "imagination" and "vision" only in connection with the artistic process and therefore as something quite apart from theology. To sever the worlds of art and theology in this way can be a serious mistake. Realizing this, critics and theologians in recent years have attempted to show how the one discipline does in fact elucidate the other.[30] But even this commendable synthesis has its dangers. Is it correct, for example, to regard the Bible as secular literature and then go on to examine the poetry of St. Mark or to analyze the entire Scripture as the embodiment of the birth-death-rebirth archetype?[31] And is it legitimate while rejecting Calvin's ideas about sin and grace to declare the *Institutes* as "one of the great and liberating acts of imagination?"[32] On the other hand, how legitimate is it for the theologian to call Picasso's "Guernica" the greatest Protestant painting in the twentieth century but say nothing about its aesthetic integrity or, conceivably, its lack of it?[33] As T. S. Eliot recognized when he questioned whether one needed to believe Dante's theology to believe his art,[34] the problem concerns the ultimate context in which the critic or the theologian conducts his respective work. If on the one hand the context is aesthetic, then certain judgments about the Bible may turn out to be grossly misleading. The same danger threatens the theologian who judges art within his own theological definitions.

In short, how can there be a meaningful union between art and theology, image and idea? The question takes us to the heart of the matter concerning what we have called the "sanctified imagination" and what we now shall call the "Christian vision." Both terms are central to an understanding of Edwards' theology.

At the outset we need to remember that in theological matters Edwards never separated sensibility from doctrine, heart from head. Were it only for his intellectualizing about religious experience he would not command the attention he receives, nor would he merit this attention were his religious feelings not also rigorously intellectual. Caricatures invariably overlook one side or the other. In Edwards' system there is an ever present inner connection, a congruence between the speculative and the affectional. This affectional side includes imagination and, beyond this, vision. Edwards not only joined sensibility and doctrine but he also shaped doctrine according to an underlying vision. Edwards' interpretation, like that of his Puritan forebears, rose from certain dictates of inspiration, certain great flashes of religious insight. This kind of theology, Perry Miller says, "dramatized the needs of the soul as does some great poem or work of art."[35] Inherent in it was what Miller calls an "Augustinian strain of piety" and a configuration more in accordance with the aesthetic vision of Augustine than the scholastic dialectics of Aquinas.[36] Miller in fact concludes important features of his interpretation of Edwards by asserting that the theologian worked "as an artist."[37]

Other students of Edwards have noted this characteristically aesthetic quality in his work. To cite only four: Samuel Perkins Hayes, early in this century, called attention to Edwards' combination of "searching irrefutable logic with a vivid oriental imagination"; Joseph Haroutunian later argued that Edwards' view of man was persistently "intellectual and aesthetic" and that his vision of the glory of God was ever stimulated and expanded by "his love for beauty in nature"; Edwin H. Cady analyzed the "artistry" in Edwards' sermon "Sinners in the Hands of an Angry God"; and Delattre has devoted an elaborate study to Edwards' aesthetics and theological ethics.[38]

In studying Edwards within this limited framework of aesthetics, it is well-nigh irresistible to acclaim him a great poet, one who stands separate from men and who, in E. M. W. Tillyard's description of a poet, inhabits "heavens and hells unbearable by the ordinary man."[39] Indeed we can see such a person in the light that Shakespeare viewed Timon of Athens: "The middle of humanity thou never knewest, but the extremity of both ends" (*Timon of Athens*, IV,iii,300-301). It was not only Edwards' intellectual might but also his gigantic heart including imagination and vision that enabled him to achieve the rare combination of clarity of thought and depth of insight. Moreover, this same combination brought vitality and concreteness to his sermons. Cast though they were in the form of cold logic, they were illumined by brilliant imagery and an underlying vision that can be called aesthetic. Finally, this aesthetic vision penetrated to heights and depths of the human spirit known only to the greatest poetic visionaries.

Yet it is not enough to call Edwards' vision "aesthetic" and to say he worked as an artist. For once again the crucial distinction needs to be made between the aesthetic and the religious, the artist and the saint. To Edwards the two sides remain separate until the redeemed heart unites them. Only when divine grace through Christ illumines the heart does the aesthetic vision become Christian, and the artist a saint. The earlier distinction between natural and sanctified imagination applies to vision. To see truly is to see through Christ; true vision is sanctified vision that apprehends God's acts in the world. From childhood Edwards himself was deeply moved by the world in which he lived; his *Personal Narrative* records the astonishing depth of feeling he achieved. He was especially moved by the sense of beauty and proportion, natural beauty serving as a "type" or emanation, however inadequate, of divine excellency. Still, there can be something faintly detached and even impersonal about such a sense, something merely aesthetic, if experience is restricted to that of beauty alone. For Edwards the total religious vision depended not only upon apprehensions of divine beauty but, supremely, upon the revelation of Christ. Edwards' supreme passion, says Haroutunian, was the glory of God not in cosmic beauty alone but in "the face of Jesus Christ."[40] Beauty apart from the face remained too abstract, the vision too general. Only in and through the face—*i.e.,* Christ's love, wisdom, humility, and saving grace—does true Christian vision obtain. This is to say that only when the total meaning of life shines forth does the aesthetic experience become the religious experience.[41] For Edwards the total meaning shone forth in the Incarnation. Christology was the touchstone of all knowledge. Edwards never assumed that the Christian believer envisions an abstract God who exists in sublime isolation as the totality and essence of beauty. Instead the believer envisions the God who comes down to man, reveals himself to man, establishes a relationship with man, face to face.

Nowhere else do the mercy and love of God appear so brightly and gloriously, said Edwards, "as they do in the face of Jesus Christ" ("Unbelievers Contemn the Glory. . . ," II,61). The meaning of this statement depends entirely upon the vision as transformed by grace. Such vision is the eye of faith by which Edwards shaped his sermons and by which he expected his congregation to hear them. Only through the eye of faith, and not the eye of flesh and blood, could his listeners behold the divine face that Edwards proclaimed. Edwards knew that imagination alone, or aesthetic vision alone, could never make understandable the distinction between the historical Jesus and the kerygmatic Christ. W. H. Auden helped to clarify this point by explaining that it is never solely through imagination that a person reconciles "the profane appearance and the sacred assertion" of one who looked like any other man, yet claimed to be the Way, the Truth, and the Life.[42] According to Auden, it is likewise impossible to behold Christ in aesthetic terms either on the stage or in visual arts. The best that a painter can do is to paint "either the Bambino with the Madonna or the dead Christ on the cross. . . . But neither a baby nor a corpse can say *I am the way,* etc."[43] In much the same tenor C. S. Lewis remarked that "the injunction to obey Christ has meaning: the injunction to obey Shakespeare is meaningless."[44] The issue concerns something beyond the dimension of aesthetics and imagination. What Edwards spoke of was a capacity to reach divine truth, to see it as it is revealed through Christ in the everyday world that all men inhabit.

In the next chapter we shall consider Edwards' theory of language as it relates to Christian imagination and vision. For now we need only emphasize Edwards' conviction that faith precedes the vision that eventuates in the word. To confuse this order is to misunderstand how Edwards related religion and words. In considering this relationship, we might ask, for example, whether Scripture is literary because it conforms to certain generic patterns, or whether the religious energies of witnessing writers shaped these patterns. Is the Biblical climax as presented in the marriage of Heaven and Earth an artistic phenomenon or a religious one? Further, is the Incarnation something created by the human imagination, or is it rather something by which the imagination is vitalized? The philosopher George Santayana exemplified this confusion by postulating that "the idea of Christ himself had to be constructed by the imagination in response to [man's] moral demands."[45] Accordingly, human imagination transformed the historical Jesus into the Christ who only as the product of a human need could accommodate human expectations. To Santayana the whole Christian doctrine is religious and efficacious "only when it becomes poetry, because only then is it the felt counterpart of personal experience and a genuine expression of human life."[46]

What Edwards would regard as insidious about this argument is the power Santayana ascribes to human imagination. Whereas Santayana attributes to it the power to transform the secular into the sacred, Edwards believed that the holy inheres in itself and needs no human instrumentality to make it so. Redemptive power belongs to God, not to man and his narratives, poetry, and myths. In truth, according to Edwards, man transforms nothing except as he himself is transformed through the power of God. Unless religious vision illumines the poet's aesthetic vision, his art will not reach the full extremities of reality, including those of divine beauty and excellency. Art will remain only art, sermons only sermons, words only words, unless infused by a prior vision that Edwards described as the "spiritual opening of the eyes in conversion" (*RA,275*). Edwards maintained that only in this way can we see the divine and supernatural light of Christ and in this light our own darkness.

Furthermore, only in this light is it possible to see redemption as a Christian "epic" (Santayana), the Incarnation as "one gigantic metaphor" (Knight), and all Biblical history as "mythological" (Kroner).[47] Whatever artistic qualities these terms signify, it is not through art but through Christ that knowledge in the Christian sense is acquired. Edwards thought of sermons as a means to such knowledge but never as *the* means. For only as Christ is known first in the heart can the Christian event be transformed into epic, metaphor, and myth. Edwards would have thought it absurd, even blasphemous, to suppose that the one-sided will of man through imagination could bring about the Christian man-God event in Christ.

In *Personal Narrative* Edwards describes the new vision that followed his conversion. He saw God in and through all things (delineated at length in *Images and Shadows of Divine Things*); he saw all things in their divine origin. "The appearance of every thing," he said, "was altered."

> God's excellency, his wisdom, his purity, and love, seemed to appear in every thing; in the sun, moon, and stars; in the clouds and blue sky; in the grass, flowers, trees; in the water and all nature; which used greatly to fix my mind. I often used to sit and view the moon for a long time; and in the day, spent much time in viewing the clouds and sky, to behold the sweet glory of God in these things: in the meantime singing forth, with a low voice, my contemplations of the Creator and Redeemer. And scarce any thing, among all the works of nature, was so sweet to me as thunder and lightning: formerly nothing had been so terrible to me. Before, I used to be uncommonly terrified with thunder, and to be struck with terror when I saw a thunder-storm rising; but now, on the contrary, it rejoiced me. I felt God, if I may so speak, at the first appearance of a thunder-storm; and used to take the opportunity, at such times, to fix myself in order to view

the clouds, and see the lightnings play, and hear the majestic and awful voice of God's thunders, which oftentimes was exceedingly entertaining, leading me to sweet contemplations of my great and glorious God. (*Personal Narrative*, I,lv)

"So far as I am concerned," Calvin wrote regarding Stephen's vision (Acts 7:55-56), "I judged that nothing was changed as to the nature of the heavens, but that Stephen was given a new sharpness of vision which, overcoming all obstacles, penetrated to the invisible Kingdom of Heaven." The unregenerate did not have the vision; it belonged only to Stephen. "From this it follows," Calvin continued, "that the miracle was wrought not in the sky, but in his eyes."[48]

For both Edwards and Calvin the miracle of vision belongs to the regenerate. All others live in the darkness of nature where unmediated paradoxes leave the human soul fractured and sight distorted. The heart, said Edwards, is the faculty that leads to synthesis, and the redeemed heart brings the beatific vision of true wholeness. However ingenious Perry Miller's argument may be—that gravity inhering within atoms (according to Newton) supplied Edwards with a "type" of the divine love that holds together all beings in the spiritual world—[49] the vision belonging to the redeemed heart is not Newtonian but Christian. With believing eyes the Christian sees the depths and heights; he sees divine origin in all things, a covenant between man and God, and redemption in history. Such was the vision that gave the Great Awakening its evangelical impulse. When the revivals ended and the vision dimmed, Edwards continued to preach, even though he suspected that what his countrymen wanted more than visions was material well-being.

CHAPTER FOUR

Religious Language

1
Opening Problems

It was not so much the weighty issues of being and nothingness that humbled young Edwards when he wrote his remarkable little essay "Of Being" before entering Yale College at the age of twelve, but rather the realization that language is not adequate to what he demanded of it. How, he wondered, does one show by words the contradiction inherent in the concept of nothingness? We cannot even talk about the contradiction "without Speaking horrid Nonsense and Contradicting our selve [sic] at every word."[1] He recognized a profound disparity between the idea of nothingness and the very act of verbalizing about it. The disparity, however, was not unique to this subject alone. As he later was to discover, it arises with any attempt to match ideas and words. Presumably he had this problem in mind when he noted in his *Diary* (in 1723) the great advantage when reading of keeping "the image and picture of the thing in mind," as if through imagination the disparity could somehow be overcome (I,lxx). Such, in fact, was his astonishing if unconscious achievement when he grappled as a child with the idea of nothingness. Impressive as his intellectual agility was at this age, we also see something of his imaginative power when he states that in order to think of nothing "we must think of the same that the sleeping Rocks Dream of."[2] Edwards was already putting to practice what later proved to be a basic insight into the nature of both knowledge and language: "to have an idea of any affection of the mind, there must be then present a degree of that affection."[3] In his later life Edwards' great task was to use words to excite affections in his readers and listeners.

The closer he came to speculating about religious matters, the more formidable the problem of language appeared. The difficulty, he said, was that "the things of Christianity are so spiritual, so refined ... so much above the things we ordinarily converse with and our common affairs for which we adapt our words" that we are forced to use words "analogically."[4] Edwards was certain that words in their literalness and "their ordinary use" do not exhibit "what we intend they should when used in divinity."[5] Yet these words had to be pressed into higher service. Somehow they had to bridge the natural and the spiritual, even though, as Edwards admitted, the world of spirit for the unenlightened appears only as so many shadows, contradictions, and paradoxes.[6] Yet Edwards knew that if Calvinism was to survive in America, the problem of religious language, co-extensive with analogical language, had to be met. For it was to the breakdown of language that he attributed "most of the jangles about religion in the world,"[7] an opinion that gives some credence to Perry Miller's assertion, even if overstated, that "New England's problem was primarily linguistic."[8] That Edwards gave priority to soul rather than language does not diminish the importance of his own linguistic problem, which, simply put, was to express the sense of the heart and through words to excite this sense in the heart of others.

The difficulty was persistently that of language. When talking about faith, for example, Edwards found no words adequate to express the act of acceptance, or what he called the "closing of the soul or heart with Christ." The word "inclination" only partially served. The same was to be said for the word "conviction." "And if we use metaphorical expressions," he went on, "such as embrace, and love, etc., they are obscure, and will not carry the same idea with them to the minds of all." All words used to express acts of the will he found at best to be only of "very indeterminate signification." "It is," he knew, "a difficult thing to find words to exhibit our own ideas."[9] When he faced the problem of defining religious affections, the keystone in his whole epistemological system, he confessed that "language is here somewhat imperfect, and the meaning of words in a considerable measure loose and unfixed" (*RA*, 97).[10] And when he referred to the ineffable object of religious affections, he quoted what became the opening words of his masterpiece: "Whom having not seen, ye love: in whom, though now ye see him not, ye rejoice with joy *unspeakable,* and full of glory" (I Peter 1:8, italics added; *RA*, 93). As writer and preacher Edwards sought words to express that joy. His was the same problem that Paul

Tillich identified with religious language: "to speak about the enigma of that which cannot be spoken";[11] or, in the words of John A. Hutchinson, to use language to deal "with an object literally out of this world."[12]

What Edwards did or did not accomplish linguistically remains an open question, one that will draw our attention later. For now we need only note that all manner of assessments have been made. His most vitriolic detractors charged that he was in a sense *too* effective, especially when describing hell and damnation; that his appalling descriptions literally frightened audiences out of their wits.[13] That his verbal pictures of heaven, hell, and God "were as real as though they had been murals painted with a brush on the gray meetinghouse walls"[14] is for other students something culturally important, the kind of Calvinist eloquence that unified New Englanders in their vision not only of the terrors that awaited backsliders but, more importantly, of the blessedness that the Church Triumphant in America would someday realize.[15] In this visionary work the evangelical preacher "was consciously and intentionally a literary artist,"[16] Edwards serving as the supreme example, the one from whose eloquence Puritan theology "blazed most clearly and most fiercely."[17] In remarking upon his language still others have called him "a singer, a poet of the past"; "a philosophical symbolist"; a writer who could have become one of "the very great names in literature" if he had not thrown himself away in service "to a particular dogma of religion."[18]

Where Edwards thought himself to stand in relation to the problems inherent in religious language is seen in his Preface to *Five Discourses* (1738), containing important sermons he preached during the Northampton revival of 1734-35. All but "Justification by Faith Alone," which he revised and expanded, appear "in that very plain and unpolished dress in which they were first prepared and delivered" (I,621). Edwards did not intend to disparage his rhetorical mastery in these five sermons. All of them—particularly "Ruth's Resolution," "The Justice of God in the Damnation of Sinners," and "The Excellency of Jesus Christ"—demonstrate great command of language. The important point is that in the Preface he enunciated a rhetorical principle he himself had adopted. The spiritual urgency of the day, he said, was enough "to make a minister neglect, forget, and despise such ornaments as politeness and modishness of style and method" (I,621). True to his Puritan inheritance, he insisted that what the times demanded was not elegance but eloquence, such as that achieved by a plain, straightforward style free from the kind of seductive tropism that had made the Anglican sermons of Jeremy Taylor and Lancelot Andrewes, to say nothing of John Donne, polished works of art rather than descriptions of spiritual reality. [19] Edwards left no doubt that his linguistic allegiance was to spiritual affections rather than to aesthetic niceties. A radical difference separated faith-language from art-language, not unlike the difference between types and tropes, the one intelligible only to persons graced with spiritual taste, the other meaningful to those with mere natural taste. To Edwards the plain style consisted of faith-language which, while no less analogical than the ornamental style he rejected, integrated its characteristics with a purpose that undergirded language itself. This purpose was to span the holy and the profane, and thereby release a spiritual eloquence that so-called aesthetic stylists dare not tamper with. Whatever such language lacked in elegance, it possessed in a more than compensatory charismatic power. With notable assurance Edwards declared that God "has been pleased to smile upon and bless a very plain unfashionable way of preaching." And have we not reason to think, he added, "that it ever has been, and ever will be, God's manner, to bless the foolishness of preaching to save them that believe, let the elegance of language and excellency of style be carried to never so great a height, by the learning and wit of the present and future ages" (I,621)?

What Edwards announced as his own plain style echoed the earlier English Puritan reaction to the tradition of pulpit elegance. John Glanvill in "A Seasonable Defence of Preaching: And the Plain Way of It" had said in 1678:

> A man doth not shew his Wit or Learning, by rolling in Metaphors, and scattering his Sentences of Greek and Latin, by abounding in high expressions, and talking in the Clouds, but he is then learned, when his learning has clear'd his Understanding, and furnish'd it with full and distinct apprehensions of things; when it enables him to make *hard* things *plain*; and conceptions, that were confused, *distinct*, and *orderly*; and he shews his learning by speaking good strong and plain Sense. [20]

Glanvill's was merely one voice articulating the principles of Petrus Ramus, the sixteenth-century French thinker who clarified the traditional trivium by distinguishing among logic ("the art of matter"), grammar ("the art of speech"), and rhetoric ("the art of the dress")—and then went on to join rhetoric to the first two, thereby constraining elegance in a manner the Puritans found much to their liking.[21] That Edwards followed in this reformed rhetorical tradition explains something of his own unerring logic and orderly style, his topical allusions to works other than Scripture, his imagery that springs with freshness and power from the content of his discourse, and his unremitting drive for spiritual truth rather than aesthetic elegance. Ramist theory and the "plain style" take one a good distance in understanding Edwards' language. Yet these explanations do not account for his effort to go beyond the poetic vision and to struggle with language befitting religious vision. Neither do they provide the insights necessary to understand his theory of religious language. For all this, we need first to go back to his reading of Locke and then to trace his independent thought and practice arising from his fundamental sense of the heart.

2

Locke's Challenge

In his youthful speculation about the nature of experience, Edwards found Lockean theories valuable, even like "handfuls of silver and gold." But, as we have seen, it was not long until he also realized their limitations, if not their downright irrelevance, in coming to terms with the separate world of religious experience. Mere sensationalism hardly shed light upon the meaning of grace, faith, and regeneration. The peculiar nature of Locke's influence seems to have been more in the questions he raised than in the answers he supplied. This is especially true of his ideas about language. For again, their value to Edwards was more in what they challenged him to work out for himself than in what they answered.

After postulating the causal relationship between sensation and ideas, Locke devoted Book III of *An Essay Concerning Human Understanding* to the subject of language. His basic premise was that words were "external" signs for "invisible ideas"; that words have no natural connection with these ideas; that words, therefore, are merely arbitrary signs or marks imposed upon ideas for the sake of common social needs (III,ii,1).[22] In any society words are simply instruments of communication. Their utility extends only as far as their significations receive common acceptance among society's members. In no way is there an inseparable connection between a word and its meaning. Since words represent "a perfect arbitrary imposition" (III,iii,8), any words will do if they are used consistently and, as it were, contractually by all persons (III,lx,2). Accordingly, the use of words becomes a matter of learning signs and their respective connections with simple ideas, substances, and what Locke called mixed modes or complex ideas. Once learned, words can signify what the user himself need never to have experienced. Children and grownups, the ignorant and the wise, can speak words "no otherwise than parrots do, only because they have learned them, and have been accustomed to those sounds" (III,ii,7). In Locke's irreversible sequence, words come after ideas (sensations) and bear only arbitrary relationships to them. Words are only words, useful to be sure, but separable from their corresponding ideas. When separated, they become like husks without the seed.

This separation is more likely to occur when words signify ideas peculiar to individual persons. Thus Locke held that words function best on the level of generalization, where they retain common meanings that everyone accepts and where they exclude what is unique to "Peter and James, Mary and Jane" (III,iii,7). In stressing the greater effectiveness of "general" words, he emphatically did not suggest that such words bear any closer connection to Peter, etc. Their effectiveness was rather in their separation from the particular, the specific, the concrete. Such general words, Locke insisted, simply do not belong to the "real existence of things" (III,iii,11). Their utility is in the fact that what they arbitrarily signify carries wider acceptance than the private significations of, say, verbal images.

Locke was unwilling to grant anything but a theoretically "perfect arbitrary imposition" of the general word upon the general idea. If this arbitrary connection broke down, it was not the fault of the word but of the idea. What Locke considered as the imperfection of language had little to do with any incapacity of one sound or another to signify an idea. In that regard, he said, "they are all equally perfect" (III,ix,4). The trouble lay with the ideas, particularly with mixed modes, as he called them, consisting of complex ideas formed by the mind itself and having no foundation in sensible experience. These mixed and abstract modes, even if widely spoken of in society, originate only as the mechanical result of the mind's tying together prior sensory experience. The singular unity of these ideas occurs as the result of the terms annexed to them. Thus "salvation," for example, is merely an arbitrarily invented term to hold what the mind by and for itself has brought together from the scattering of prior sensations. Whereas the sensations (simple ideas) have a basis in nature, the collection that the mind shapes does not. This is not to say that Locke denied the validity of such ideas. But he did emphasize that the mind alone makes the so-called collection (mixed mode), and that the term (*e.g.*, "salvation") is "the knot" that ties the loose parts together (III,v,10).

We see, then, that for Locke words are merely words, terms merely terms, having no natural or inherent meaning, no necessary connection with anything beyond themselves. As counters, any imperfections they sustain must be traced back to the obscurity of the ideas with which they are linked. If words are insignificant, the blame finally rests with those who use them without any clear understanding of what they signify. Locke's target now comes into focus. If the abusers of words were asked what "wisdom, glory, grace, etc." mean, Locke said, they would not know what to answer—"a plain proof" that "though they have learned those sounds, and have them ready at their tongue's end, yet there are no determined ideas laid up in their minds, which are to be expressed to others by them" (III,x,3). His target clearly identified, Locke went on to denounce those persons who utter words that signify "unsteady and confused notions." The worst of these offenders, whose language deteriorates to "unintelligible noise and jargon," are those who speculate about "moral matters" (III,x,4). Locke's salvoes were aimed specifically at those persons who talk about religion: the "learned disputants," "these all-knowing doctors," "the parson of the parish" whose "learned gibberish" is full of sound and fury signifying nothing that really exists in nature (III,x,8-9,16).

Locke's solution was as simple as it was logical. Words must have their prior ideas. Even if these ideas be as complex as justice, grace, and salvation, Locke believed they can be possessed and expressed with exactness. As "merchants and lovers, cooks and taylors, have words wherewithal to dispatch their ordinary affairs, . . . so, I think, might philosophers and disputants too, if they had a mind to understand and to be clearly understood" (III,xi,10). Taking comfort in the serene logicality of language and the "perfect" arbitrariness with which words are affixed to ideas, Locke had only to summarize his argument by affirming that because morality is as capable of demonstration as mathematics, and because "the precise real essence of the things moral words stand for may be perfectly known," a perfect harmony can likewise exist between the word and the idea when social convention stamps one upon the other (III,xi,16).

On one level Locke's analysis struck Edwards as entirely valid. Both men recognized the deterioration of language that takes place when words lose their anchorage in ideas. Both knew that as a consequence people mouth empty words. Perhaps, however, even empty words served a certain social expediency; for indeed, as Edwards obliquely suggested, a person's rate of reading would become intolerably slow if he were bothered to connect such words as God, man, people, misery, happiness, salvation, sanctification, to ideas he presumably held in his mind.[23] Furthermore, what if he were required to experience the "actual idea," involving the full range of feeling and passion, before he moved on to the next word! Even Locke had declared that if connections with ideas are made too privately by Peter, James, Mary, and Jane, such words lose their meaning anyway. His implication was clearly that if language remains public and general it provides at least quasi-communication; and if social convention nicely fixes words to ideas, then the utility of language conceivably becomes perfected. Locke was satisfied that the mere cognition of a word takes one mechanically back to its idea if the two are properly fixed. He did not ask for any apprehension of the idea itself.

As suggested, Edwards was impressed with Locke's explanation of the way language deteriorates. He too observed that words are sometimes only signs that substitute for ideas. Very commonly, he said, we discourse about things "without any idea at all of the things themselves in any degree, but only make use of the signs instead of the ideas."[24] When, for example, we think of such abstractions as man, nations, conversion, conviction, we commonly have only confused notions, and are content to use external signs instead of seeking those apprehensions that properly represent the ideas. Edwards saw that the obvious challenge on this level was to attach words to ideas once again.

But Locke had unwittingly presented a greater challenge—unwittingly, because, unlike Edwards, he failed to recognize that words necessarily lose their anchorage when they are only artificially secured in the first place. In short, Edwards knew that words are destined to their willy-nilly way unless they are grounded in "actual ideas." The real task that Locke left with Edwards was not only to join word and idea but somehow to unite knowledge and being, cognition and apprehension, and to conceive of words not as arbitrary signs but as existential events. Here was a level of language Locke never touched, except to keep such poles forever apart. But Locke's failure was Edwards' challenge, and thus Locke's primary influence was not as a model but as a goad.

Contrary to Locke, Edwards based his theory of language upon actual human existence, always personal, concrete, subjective. Locke had said that words do not belong to the real existence of things. Edwards held that it was exactly there where they do belong. Unless their roots anchor there, words will forever remain the mere external counters that Locke said they were. The crucial point rests with what Edward meant by actual ideas as being inseparable from human existence.

> To have an actual idea of a thought is to have that thought, that we have an idea of, then in our minds. To have an actual idea of any pleasure or delight, there must be excited a degree of that delight; so to have an actual idea of any trouble or kind of pain, there must be excited a degree of that pain or trouble; and to have an idea of any affection of the mind, there must be then present a degree of that affection.[25]

The key point shows Edwards to be in an entirely different realm of speculation from that of Lockean sensationalism. He conceived of language as involving something more than the connection with mixed modes mechanically formed from simple ideas of sensation, and certainly something more than the cognitive knowledge such modes represented. To Edwards language is connected to actual ideas. To have an actual idea of something is itself an experience; it is an apprehension, "a direct ideal view or contemplation of the thing thought of."[26] Apprehension may pertain to the faculty of understanding or to what Edwards figuratively called the head. But apprehension also pertains to the will, to what he figuratively called the heart, and it was in reference to this realm that he used the expression "having a sense." By it he meant "some feeling of the heart."[27] This is sensible, not cognitive knowledge; but it is sensible knowledge in the Edwardsean and not Lockean usage. That Edwards identified the distinction between speculative and sensible knowledge as "the most important of all" distinctions[28] —one that may well be thought to represent "Edwards' most important achievement"[29] —fails to do full justice to Edwards' insight unless we come finally to recognize that sensible knowledge does not mean, as it did for Locke, mere sensory experience that the mind, apart from emotions, weaves together into mixed modes and then seals with a linguistic term. Sensible knowledge for Edwards meant heart-knowledge, an apprehension that enlists the emotions and finally the totality of being itself. It must be emphasized, therefore, that whatever linguistic problems Locke laid before Edwards, their solution required of Edwards something more than Locke's own principles. Edwards was convinced that the basis of language must be existential, a tying of words to experience and a sending of living stuff into them. Like fruit to the vine, words have their life only in their final oneness with the heart.

3

Limitations of Language

In spite of all his complex speculations, Edwards inevitably designed his strands so that they either originated from or found their destination in the human heart and its sense of things. Never is this point more certain than in his conception of language as inseparable from the core of existence. Whether, therefore, he thought of language as emanating from the heart or as aimed towards it, he saw an underlying unity existing between word and heart.

This relationship becomes doubly significant when we remember that what Edwards meant by heart was, ultimately, the capacity to sense divine excellency, to apprehend spiritual things. This capacity had nothing to do with the limiting sensationalism of Locke, to whom sense experience involved the five natural senses. What Edwards meant was something entirely different, "a new inward perception or sensation . . . a new spiritual sense that the mind had, or a principle of a new kind of perception or spiritual sensation, which is in its whole nature different from any former kinds of sensation" (*RA*,205-206). Edwards' reference here is to a different *manner* of perceiving. But what of the perceptions themselves, the *matter?* They too are new: "So that the spiritual perceptions which a sanctified and spiritual person has, are not only diverse from all that natural men have, after the manner that the ideas or perceptions of the same sense may differ one from another, but rather as the ideas and sensations of different sense do differ" (*RA*,206). The perceptions are those of a new reality. In its fullest meaning, therefore, a sense of the heart combines manner and matter. With new eyes we see a new reality, and this fullness is the work of the Spirit of God.

Even though Edwards could speak of the "sanctified" person, he did not apply the same term to language for the simple reason that language, though inseparable from the heart, is neither (1) the means of regeneration nor (2) the adequate testimony of it. He could more justifiably speak of sanctified imagination and vision, insofar as such capacities are subsumed within the condition from which they take their meaning. Nevertheless, as we have said, Edwards understood the importance of joining language and emotion. Much of New England's religious apathy he traced to the cleavage between the two. If, he reasoned, the word as mere sign is dead, if it lacks connection with idea, then "we are put to the trouble of exciting the actual idea and making it as lively and clear as we can."[30] This notion represents an important departure from Locke's view that experience precedes language. By contrast, Edwards conceived of language as a way to excite experience, and suggested that a speaker's ability to excite actual ideas measures his "force and strength."[31]

An important caveat enters at this point, namely, that words cannot excite the actual idea of, say, salvation. Here, then, is the first limitation that Edwards accepted as inherent in theological language. Words do not cause the light; neither do they imbue the heart with religious affections. Although he held that words do convey doctrine or the "subject matter" of the light, he never took the next step to suggest that they properly cause either the manner or matter of sanctified perception.[32] We see, therefore, that even though language excites experience and transmits doctrine, there must be some power beyond and outside language that excites religious experience. Assimilating words and all their rhetorical potential does not cause the reader to behold truth. The notion of words as the *occasional* cause and not as the *efficient* cause underlies Perry Miller's accurate observation that "after the artist [or preacher] has provided the verbal environment [the occasional cause], at this point another power [the efficient cause] must intervene if the beholder is to collect out of it the conception."[33] That other power is the Spirit of God through grace. What Edwards recognized with great conviction was that theological terms such as salvation, faith, sin, judgment, covenant, plus any rhetorical embellishments a preacher might add, do not take the listener to the final truth locked within these notions unless divine grace has first empowered his heart to sense that which the language signifies. Only after this event does theological vocabulary become religious language, and only then did Edwards consider such language and the redeemed heart as one.

A second limitation that Edwards identified with theological language is its inadequacy to express the sense of the heart, even when as religious language it originates therein. The problem in this instance is that language cannot contain and express a true sense of the speaker's own antecedent experience. Although this problem gives rise to the kind of linguistic frustrations Edwards repeatedly confessed to, it contains nothing hazardous unless a person thinks that language is indeed adequate. In such a case, he may suppose that any limitations in language can be transcended through contrivance, perhaps through sheer exhortation or aesthetic creativeness. Actually, Edwards argued, the problem is not the limitation of language at all but the failure of persons to recognize the paradox that limitation is itself a positive quality that helps to establish the primacy of that greater power which limits language. To regard limitation, on the contrary, as something to overcome with even more language led to what Edwards clearly saw as the delusion of exhortation and its "ostentatious" practitioners (*RA*,135). To go even further and suppose that language is inspired by the same grace that touches the heart is the way of "hypocrites" who claim the power of their rhetoric to be equal to or one with that of grace. Edwards realized that "to be fluent, fervent and abundant, in talking of the things of religion" may in fact be only the "religion of the mouth and of the tongue," not of the heart (*RA*,135,136). He suspected with subtle and yet telling insight that "false affections, if they are equally strong, are much more forward to declare themselves, than true" (*RA*,137).

Isn't it contradictory, we might ask, that America's foremost preacher, who brought religious language to consummate heights, should declare that true religious affections are *less* forward to declare themselves than are false? I think not. What Edwards learned about the nature of such language is that its very limitations testify to the gracious but separate power that first touches the heart of him who speaks and writes it. In this regard there is a stunning similarity between Edwards and Kierkegaard, and, at the same time, an equally decisive refutation of those who insist upon calling Edwards a great artist. For both Kierkegaard and Edwards the true sense of the heart is conveyed by one's life, not by one's words. It was for good reason that of his twelve "Distinguishing Signs of Truly Gracious and Holy Affections," Edwards devoted (in *Religious Affections*) his chief attention to the last one, "Christian practice," which takes up one-third of the total discussion. But more importantly, both men knew that if a person aspires to religious knowledge, he will have to discover that the prerequisite is a transformed heart and a giving up of everything for its sake. Kierkegaard believed that for the poet this means relinquishing his art, and, in what would be analogous for the preacher, giving up his "artistic" sermon. Once a poet experiences religious vision, once he exists religiously, he either stops writing or regards words as incidental, even as accidental. A prolific writer himself, Kierkegaard rejected the creative life. An eloquent preacher, Edwards spurned a self-conscious artistry. For both men the point of reference was God, not aesthetic beauty. If, according to Kierkegaard, a poet seeks to establish a relation to the religious through his natural imagination, "he succeeds only in establishing an aesthetic relation to something aesthetic." If, on the other hand, the poet through grace lives in a relationship to the religious, if in truth the religious is the religious, then he will know that true existence "does not consist in singing and hymning and composing verses." Kierkegaard then noted that if the poet's productivity "does not cease entirely, or if it flows as richly as before, [it] comes to be regarded by the individual himself as something *accidental.*"[34]

Again, Kierkegaard's emphasis rests with the point of reference: if it is beauty, then what is essential is poetic productivity, not the mode of existence; if, on the other hand, it is God, then existence within this relationship is essential and words are only "accidental." Another way of viewing this Kierkegaardian distinction is to say that whereas art seeks to preserve, stabilize, and imbue with significance man's experience, religion shows the inadequacy of the human as an explanation of the way things are, and instead forces an alien vision upon man, undermines him, and finally discloses meaning only as he relates to the disclosure.[35] Thus it follows that art presupposes the stability of the human word, religion presupposes the opposite. Art implies the unity, coherence, and radiance of the word, however incomplete. But precisely because the word is incomplete, religion implies a fuller Word in another realm.

Perry Miller approaches the same conclusion in positing that "if Edwards' artistry was an accidental effect or a consequence of real passion [grace], it would be genuine"—*i.e.*, genuine religious language that springs from true religious affections, not artistic or theological language.[36] Miller did not go on to remove his conditional "if." Perhaps it is not essential that anyone does. What is essential for an understanding of Edwards' theory of language as well as his rhetoric is to realize that when related to the gracious heart, language is necessarily subordinate. To interpret Edwards as a self-conscious artist and an "artistic" pulpit orator[37] may miss the fundamental point that for him language is accidental to truly gracious and holy affections. According to Edwards' theory, if a person would seek to express the true sense of these affections, he must let the seed break open the husk; let the "holy ardour" of the heart transform the words so as to make them invisible in the greater light;[38] let language become like that of Augustine, who according to Richard Kroner always wrote "in a prayerful mood." "If ever an author was a man of grace," Kroner said, "Augustine was that man."[39] A similar judgment regarding Kierkegaard and Edwards may not be amiss, if by this judgment we mean that the experience of religion rather than the strategy of rhetoric accounted for the ardor of their language—an ardor that made their words accidental.[40]

As we have noted, the two limitations Edwards found inherent in language, even in the religious language of the heart, were (1) that words alone can never serve as the means of grace and (2) that words are never adequate to express gracious feelings. Contrary to the myth generated by countless critics and detractors who have regarded Edwards as a Samson of rhetoric whose power lay in his words, Edwards applied these limits to his own practice and, moreover, converted them into warnings for others.

In the first place he warned against making words the foundation of Christian belief and affection. Words, including those of Scripture, are "occasional" instruments; they are indispensable in preparing the recipient for the saving and comprehensive idea of Christian love. But they are never the foundation and cause of this love, even if certain words should seem to burn one in some sudden and inexplicable way. Edwards spared no force in denouncing those persons who claimed words to be revelations and who therefore were given to quoting them. All the sense such Bible-quoters and thumpers have of any glory in words is only from "self-love, and from their own imagined interest in the words" (RA,221). Their being affected with this imagined interest was clear evidence to Edwards of "the wretched delusion" they were under (RA,221).

Even while we notice Edwards' adherence to Biblical texts in his sermons, we are misled if we think he regarded Biblical words as the means by which God "speaks" to men as in some kind of divine conversation. In repudiating any such notion, he argued that when persons regard words borne into their thoughts as suddenly spoken by God through Scripture, they are guilty of "a blind application," belonging "to the spirit of darkness, and not of light" (*RA,225*). Such an application might be that of a soldier in a trench who, after reading words from the Bible, claims to have received God's promise to be spared in the next enemy attack. The soldier's delusion is in the particularity of the promise, as if the Biblical words were those of God speaking only to him at that instant. Edwards would argue that the soldier has substituted a covenant of Biblical words for the covenant of grace that encompasses all promises and is founded not upon words at all but upon Christ.

Edwards warned that words, like sand, provide no foundation for faith. They are not the "efficient" means of it. They do not excite the saving sense of God's glory. Any strategy designed to have them do so—to have them weave, for example, some incantatory spell in order that the mind be infused with a sense of the supernatural—he considered dangerous deception. Words indeed prepare the mind for a sense of God's glory. They herald something like an aesthetic vision of it. But they emphatically do not reach the religious vision of it nor can they incarnate it. True joy remains unspeakable. Not words but grace enables one to reach this level, and its only incarnation is Christ.

This makes evident Edwards' other warning, directed to those persons who suppose their utterances to emanate from a gracious heart when in fact they arise only from a lively imagination. The distinction here is between revelation and inspiration as the source of language. Edwards cautioned that whereas revelation is the wellspring of religious language, such language is never adequate to convey the sense of it. Those who suppose that it is unwittingly infer inspiration as its source. However inadequate they are, words that spring from revelation contain its truth; on the other hand, words that arise from inspiration, independent of any antecedent revelation, actually suggest "new truths and doctrines" which when taken as religious insights must necessarily be only human delusions ("Divine and Supernatural Light," II,13). The one kind of rhetoric is characterized by simplicity and humility; the other, by embellishment and pride. Thus, the substance of Edwards' warnings stems from his conviction that religious language reaches the heart only if grace has reached it first; and, if grace *has* reached it, the heart does not require words for its full expression.

4

Language as "Occasional" Cause

The limitations of religious language did not prevent Edwards from carrying language far beyond the restrictions Locke had placed upon it. To Edwards the Lockean theory meant that only one room of the mind—cognition—was being served, whereas he based his whole epistemological theory upon the primacy of that other room, apprehension. For words to serve here, they had to be commensurate with the mind's capacity to apprehend ideas. This mode of knowledge involved not only intellect but emotion; and for words to serve this capacity they had to excite the *actual* idea, the feelings, the deep and private foundations of true knowledge, the "sense" of things rather than the mere cognition of them. To reiterate, Edwards never carried language to the point where it served to excite the actual idea of redemption. He never considered language to be the means of or the substitute for God's power through grace. Nevertheless, for him language did have important work to do.

On the literal level language conveys the facts and circumstances of doctrine. That Edwards sought to apprehend the "sense" of language on a deeper, experiential level did not nullify his insistence upon straightforward doctrinal language. With every sermon he presupposed this foundation. The "subject matter" of the word first had to be heard. Unless doctrine was firmly in the mind, the spiritual light of the word, its true excellency and meaning, could not be known ("Divine and Supernatural Light," II,15). It bears repeating that in no way did Edwards suppose the word outside of grace to cause the light; he recognized the limits of language well enough. But he did want the "notion of doctrines in our heads" as well as "the sense of divine excellency of them in our hearts" (II,15). He had no intention of circumventing denotative and doctrinal meaning.

But even a cursory reading of Edwards' sermons convinces a person of something more than their intellectual content and precision. His sermons reached out to another dimension: to what he called "double signification,"[41] the external meaning heard by the ear and understood by the head, and the internal meaning heard and felt by the heart. Double signification was an idea he substantiated more in practice than in theory. We notice, however, that he was not

satisfied, for example, with the Rev. John Taylor's literalism in
Scripture-Doctrine of Original Sin (1738), and said, in opposition to
Taylor, that such words as death, naked, light, heart, discovery,
sense, do "truly and properly signify other things of a more spiritual
internal nature."[42] Edwards engaged in long exposition on the word
"death" to show that its single meaning (*i.e.,* the loss of this present
life), which Taylor had settled for, failed to touch the multiple
nuances of connotative or double signification. If, as Edwards
thought, the unregenerate were deaf to the heart-word, they might
at least be awakened to a deeper human level than that of ratiocination and literalism. Edwards was convinced that language had the
"natural force or influence" to excite feelings (II,15). Even if they
were not those of true religious affections, such natural feelings may
be proper to and in harmony with these affections. In this sense
Edwards believed that language created in the listener and reader an
emotional readiness necessary for the apprehension of religious
truth.

From this pivotal point we see Edwards' theory of language taking
final shape. At one extreme he rejected Locke's view of language as
being too restrictive, too mechanical, and arbitrary; at the other
extreme he recognized the inherent limitations of religious language
to either effect or express God's grace. There remained, however, an
important area in which language could usefully serve religious ends.
Up to a point language could induce experiences appropriate to
religious insight. As John Witherspoon declared in his lectures on
"Eloquence" delivered at Princeton in the late 1760's, the excellence
of eloquence consisted "in making another perceive what I perceive,
and feel towards it as I feel."[43] The test of the preacher's power was
in whether he could transform doctrine into preparatory experience
that grace would complete as saving experience. This test was the
crucial premise in Edwards' rhetoric. Like other Calvinist preachers
of the Great Awakening, he affirmed the reality of religious vision
and believed that the description of it would induce appropriate
feelings within his hearers. His descriptions were not intended as
aesthetic surrogates for religious reality, nor as entertainment for the
imagination. Instead they were to describe what in truth existed
even though seen as only through a glass darkly—yet not darkly

either, for Edwards believed that what the sanctified imagination beheld was far more brightly illumined than what the natural eye could see.

Language, therefore, was the preliminary means of applying religious truths to the heart. When used eloquently, it gave form and content to insights concerning judgment, damnation, and hell, the resurrection of the just, and divine history. Language furnished the heart with feelings preparatory to revelation.

Edwards' belief that the aim of language, and thus the sermon, is to prepare the heart to embrace both the divine promise and the divine promiser implied something special about the nature of language in its penultimate role. To identify this ingredient we might suggest, with Justus George Lawler, that words are like icebergs, which have most of their surface below water—or like prisms, containing all the colors even though some remain invisible.[44] There is something in words, apart from their one-dimensional meaning, that compares with the invisible dimension of the iceberg and prism, some power of double signification that awakens us, as Wordsworth said in his Intimation Ode, not only to the literal light but also to the "celestial light" and "visionary gleam." Lawler calls this other dimension of the word the "daimonic," its soul and power. To regard the word as mere sign, or the sermon as intellectual dialectic, is to miss this inner core of language. But to experience the word as image, to perceive its vital core as taking form in metaphor and symbol, is to pass from uninterpreted meaning to transformed meaning. "Only what stands before our eyes as image, as form, as figure, has meaning for us; only that confronts us as power," says Gerardus van der Leeuw.[45]

There is no suggestion here that Edwards embraced the kind of image-making that Roman Catholics practiced and Calvin denounced. Both Edwards and Calvin turned away from man-made representations of the Deity, whether in timber, stone, gold, silver, or the verbal arts.[46] Yet Calvin was a man of the Renaissance before he was a Reformer. In his hands French prose took on an exactness and strength that made it a vehicle for theological writing of the highest order.[47] A similar energy, steady coherence, and architectonic grandeur distinguish Edwards' style. He assigned great value to words. Like Calvin, he enlivened his prose with the kind of sensory detail and surging cadences that quickened readers to something like spiritual awareness, whether it was of God's wrath or of his mercy.[48] His figurative language served to point towards something beyond. Typological connection required that that something first "take place." For Edwards the reality takes place when the inner energy of the word issues forth through such images as light, darkness, fire, and tempest. To arrive at this invisible dimension within the word, to experience it with feeling and passion, the reader must enter into what has been imaged forth. This entrance can be the aesthetic initiation, as it were, into what resembles or harmonizes with the religious situation to follow. As Herbert Read points out, an aesthetic awareness of space prepares a person for a religious awareness of transcendence.[49] Yet we must again emphasize that the aesthetic experience is not *the* means to the religious, nor does it stand in some kind of logical relationship to it, as if the latter were the consequence of the former. In Edwards, as in Calvin, there always remained the radical distinction between the human and the divine, between aesthetics and religion, between "earthly things" and "heavenly things."[50] To call attention to Edwards' artistic style, and to see his language for what it legitimately is, we need to draw up a kind of working dictum that states: Although an aesthetic dimension exists in religion, religion is something more than aesthetics, aesthetics something less than religion. In van der Leeuw's terms, beauty is holiness but holiness is not wholly beauty.[51]

As for the linguistic area lying between arbitrary signs and holy unspeakableness, Edwards demonstrated that words could indeed bring things to life if not to divine light. He did not mistake words for the excellency towards which they pointed, nor did he construe language as the *a priori* cause of our apprehending this excellency. After all, words were words. But unlike Locke he knew that they were inseparable from the emotions to be both transmitted and evoked. Like Tillich, he thought of words as opening up transcendent levels of reality and unlocking depths within ourselves.[52] Most importantly, he believed that as language succeeds in quickening us to these dimensions within and beyond, it has done its work in preparing the heart for the gracious light.

5
The Sermon

It would seem that rigidly structured sermons could hardly have been expected to warm the heart. Unlike Anglican sermons, which allowed for broader expansion and all manner of artistic filigree, those preached in New England by Edwards' ancestors were encased in an outline that invariably started with the *text* and *doctrine,* then mechanically led to *reasons* or *proofs,* and ended with *uses.* Each of these sections was divided, with each subdivision clearly numbered or lettered and each topic explicitly defined, so that when the sermon appeared on the printed page it looked, in Miller's opinion, "more like a lawyer's brief than a work of art."[53] These sermons, of course, were never intended as works of art, and to read them as such only restores the confusion between art and religion already discussed. Miller's subsequent turnabout sets the matter correctly:

> Upon reviewing the results of our study [of Puritan sermon style], we might reflect that any criticism which endeavors to discuss Puritan writings as part of literary history, which seeks to estimate them from an 'aesthetic' point of view, is approaching the materials in a spirit they were never intended to accommodate, and is in danger of concluding with pronouncements which are wholly irrelevant to the designs and motives of the writers.[54]

This statement puts the sermon into a different class from that of literature. The aim of the sermon was not that of art. If the preacher achieved an artistic level, he did so not as an end in itself but as the means by which to convey religious understanding to the mind and religious warmth to the heart. The rigid three-part form was not antithetical to this objective. Plain doctrinal statements based on Biblical texts, followed by the intellectual reinforcement of the doctrine, thus prepared the congregation for the application which necessarily concerned the heart, will, and religious affections.

The sermon was neither a strict *tour de force* in logic nor some kind of artistic emotional appeal meant to lure people into agony or ecstasy devoid of intellectual content.[55] Avoiding the pitfalls of either extreme, Edwards regarded the sermon as a "fit means" for impressing "divine things on the hearts and affections" (*RA,*115). It conveyed to sinners the importance of religion, their own spiritual misery, the need for remedy, and the glory and sufficiency of the remedy. On the other hand, it stirred the hearts of saints and quickened their affections. Always the overwhelming purpose was to convey the meaning of religious life. This required, first, a logical exposition of doctrine to which listeners were to respond with intellectual *conviction,* and, second, an experiential and immediate "sense" of divinity to which they were to respond with willing *consent.* Even though the first step gave way to the second, Edwards accorded it its due proportion, warning fellow preachers against "inspiration" aimed at short-circuiting study and sound doctrinal analysis.

During the Connecticut Valley revivals, he frequently admonished ministers of the dangers that accompanied both extremes. To clergymen whose enthusiasm led them and their congregations into sheer emotionalism, he warned never to despise "human learning" and the careful attention to reason in their doctrinal handling of religious matters (*Distinguishing Marks,*282). Whenever spontaneity replaced careful study, Edwards grew suspicious that more heat than light was being generated. He cautioned against "too much heat" and "angry zeal," which Arminian detractors were wont to single out to attack (*Distinguishing Marks,*287). However, to those ministers who withheld their support of the Awakening, who preached in what he considered a moderate, dull, indifferent way, or who paid inordinate attention to intellectual abstraction, Edwards uttered warnings of equal importance. "Our people," he said, "don't so much need to have their heads stored, as to have their hearts touched; and they stand in the greatest need of that sort of preaching that has the greatest tendency to do this" (*Thoughts,*388). If touching their hearts meant describing their "infinitely miserable condition," if it meant speaking of the true hell their congregations were afraid to see for themselves, then Edwards encouraged his compatriots "to take great pains to make men sensible of it" (*Distinguishing Marks,*247). Why should the people not be told the truth, he urged, even if such truth destroys their peace. Since their peace is only that which natural men enjoy, a peace and comfort founded in darkness, it behooves ministers to shed light, even if, in such light, peace vanishes and congregations are terrified. Edwards advised the surgeon to lance the boil regardless of the pain.

In all his advice to fellow preachers, his favorite metaphor remained that of light—an important metaphor throughout his theological writing. According to James Carse, it carried the twofold meaning of penetration and action: light as knowledge that enters the darkness of man's mind, and light as a way of perceiving truth. [56] In the first instance, light is the knowledge of God that only God gives; in the second, it is the state of spiritual enlightenment in which we see true meaning. [57] Edwards dramatically applied the metaphor to preachers, charging them to be burning and shining lights amid the false light of reason and science. By 1742 the controversies of the Enlightenment had diminished much of the revival's intensity. In the same year, Edwards declared: "We had need to be as full of light as a glass is, that is held out in the sun" (*Thoughts*, 507). He repeated the summons two years later in "The True Excellency of a Gospel Minister," a sermon delivered at the ordination of the Rev. Robert Abercrombie. Nothing else Edwards wrote surpassed his description here of false piety—and then of the true piety that he hoped would illumine the gospel minister. The passage also serves to illustrate Edwards' linguistic theory in practice: the word as experience.

> Where there is light in a minister, consisting in human learning, great speculative knowledge and the wisdom of this world, without a spiritual warmth and ardour in his heart, and a holy zeal in his ministrations, his light is like the light of an *ignis fatuus*, and some kinds of putrifying carcasses that shine in the dark, though they are of a stinking savour. And if on the other hand a minister has warmth and zeal, without light, his heat has nothing excellent in it, but is rather to be abhorred; being like the heat of the bottomless pit; where, though the fire is great, yet there is no light. To be hot in this manner, and not lightsome, is to be like an angel of darkness. But ministers having light and heat united in them, will be like the angels of light; which for their light and brightness are called morning stars. (II,958)

Sustaining the metaphor, he concludes:

> . . . we are set by Christ to be lights or luminaries in the spiritual world. . . . We shall be like Christ, and shall shine with his beams; Christ will live in us, and be seen in his life and beauty in our ministry. . . . In this way, those whom Christ has set to be lights in his church, and to be stars in the spiritual world here, shall be lights also in the church triumphant, and shine as stars forever in heaven. (II,959)

Redemptive transformation of the heart brings new life to both imagination and language. Within the divine and supernatural light, the heart releases, as it were, a new vision and a new language.

Edwards affirmed that Christian ministers, through their sermons, can prepare the hearts of listeners and readers for redemption eventuating in similar vision. Of foremost importance was that these ministers awaken their people to the great Christian experiences (and doctrines) of sin and salvation. Towards this great effort Edwards directed his own preaching. Grasped by "conviction" and inclined by "consent," he saw himself as a visible light given power by God's invisible grace. His vision and language, empowered by the greater light, testify to the mighty proportions of his own religious life.

CHAPTER FIVE

Sin

1
Pulpit Language

After Edwards left Northampton in 1751 to begin his duties in the frontier village of Stockbridge, he was invited to preach before the Synod of New York, which on this occasion (Sept. 28, 1752) convened at Newark, New Jersey. The controversies over religious experience, the Half-Way Covenant, qualifications for communion, and the circumstances of his dismissal from his Northampton pulpit had not yet ended, although their jagged immediacy had abated simply because he was now removed from the scene. On this occasion he chose for his text James 2:19—"Thou believest that there is one God; thou doest well: the devils also believe, and tremble." The sermon typified Edwards' careful way through the subtleties of his subject, in this case the deceptive resemblances between sinners and saints. After expanding upon these resemblances, intended to jolt his listeners into examining themselves, he laid down three "sure signs" of the saving grace of God's Spirit—namely, *foundation, tendency,* and *exhortation.* Foundation pertained to the believer's "sense of divine beauty"; tendency, to his redirection in humility and love; and exhortation, to his "communication of something of God's own beauty and excellency" ("True Grace Distinguished. . . ," II,48-50). Edwards concluded by saying about those saints in whom all three signs converge:

> . . . however they may now wander in a wilderness, or be tossed to and fro on a tempestuous ocean, they [shall] certainly arrive in heaven at last, where this heavenly spark shall be increased and perfected, and the souls of the saints all be transformed into a bright and pure flame, and they shall shine forth as the sun in the kingdom of their Father. (II,50)

For all their visionary brilliance the autobiographical overtones of this passage reinforce the importance Edwards accorded language— the third and special gift, he said, that God bestows "only on his

115

special favourites" (II,50). As we have seen, it was to the subject of language that Edwards directed his speculation about religious experience, imagination, and vision. It was the connection between heart and word that gave him the basis for positing a religious language, however limited. The importance assigned to language he justified not in Lockean terms of social convention but in experiential terms of the heart: words as indistinguishable from actual ideas that men feel; words as "occasional cause," preparation, environment—all evoking feelings harmonious with religious affections. Finally, it was upon the preacher that the responsibility of language rested with particular significance. Endowed with the gift of exhortation after he had received a new foundation in Christ and tendency in love, the preacher became a burning light to dispel the darkness of sin and unite with the light of salvation. The metaphor of light conjoined with the act of sight: Edwards wanted people to see the light, and in seeing it to become it. The gospel minister was such a light. His language communicated its felt presence, not as something created by lively imagination or fancy but as truth, fact, revelation.

Thus the language of the sermon consisted in something more than "plain style." As conceived by Edwards, it could better be described as "pure style" in which the idea is not only connected but consolidated with the word, so that the one is expressible only in terms of the other.[1] The word is the perception.

In reading Edwards' sermons one needs to pay attention to more than speculative theology and literary technique. Terms like "precision," "exactitude," "vividness," "intricacy" do indeed describe his multi-level style.[2] But unless one also notices the synthesis of clear argument and the quickening spirit of direct experience, the convergence of "information and inspiration,"[3] one has not read his sermons in their real fullness. To do this one needs to read them within the same vision that first impelled them. The reader must recognize their implicit typological analogies between physical things and spiritual truths, between finite and Infinite Being.[4] Furthermore, to read them this way involves not only reading the word as image—be it, say, the image of light or darkness—but somehow the actualization of what one has read, at that moment when the word is literally the event.

Much has been written about Edwards' pulpit style. "He had the power of inspired appeal and exhortation," said Alexander V. G. Allen in his study of Edwards.[5] He used "scriptural and popular imagery with perfect honesty," observes Haroutunian, adding that Edwards was honest enough to know that conceptions of heaven and hell taken from the world of sense were "hopelessly inadequate" to describe the infinite fullness of supernatural realities.[6] Perry Miller looks upon Edwards' pulpit oratory as "a consuming effort to make sounds become objects, to control and discipline his utterance so that words would immediately be registered on the sense not as noises but as ideas." Accordingly, Edwards had to "*make* words convey the idea of heaven" and "*force* them to give the idea of hell."[7] In Winslow's concise assessment, Edwards sought "to make scriptural preachment a reality."[8]

These appraisals indicate that what Edwards sought to achieve through language was consistent with what he conceived to be the true function of language. When he advised fellow ministers about their own pulpit oratory, his consistency did not waver. They show the "best kindness" to their congregation, he said, when they "represent ... the truth of the case" and set it forth in the "liveliest manner" (*Distinguishing Marks,*247). Whether the truth pertains to sin or to salvation, whether it describes the natural or the regenerate man, those who care for souls were to take "great pains" to make people sensible of it. If the truth be that of hell itself, Edwards' call was to preach it! With faultless logic and vivid language he declared: "I think it is a reasonable thing to endeavor to fright persons away from hell, that stand upon the brink of it, and are just ready to fall into it, and are senseless of their danger: 'tis a reasonable thing to fright a person out of an house on fire" (*Distinguishing Marks,*248).

It must be said at once that Edwards never encouraged the preaching of terror for its own sake.[9] As we shall notice when we examine his "Sinners in the Hands of an Angry God," certain critics have so outrageously caricatured him as to suggest that his pleasure in preaching hellfire increased in ratio to his listeners' pain. On the contrary, Edwards specifically warned against terrifying with what was not true, or with what did not invite "the weary and the heavy laden to their Savior" ("The True Excellency of a Gospel Minister," II,957). More importantly, he warned against preaching what ministers had not themselves **experienced** (*Thoughts,*506-507). Searching one's own heart was always a prerequisite for preaching to the hearts of others. Implicit in all Edwards' sermons about damnation were his own vast regions of feeling, his own torment and sense of hell. To grasp the full impact of these hellfire sermons, the reader needs to place them alongside Edwards' *Personal Narrative,* in which he cried out, "When I look into my heart, and take view of my wickedness, it looks like an abyss infinitely deeper than hell" (I,xc). For Edwards the infinite stretched in both directions, and to preach of effulgent light presupposed the knowledge of infinite darkness. He preached with great solemnity concerning all these things, his voice "a little languid, with a note of pathos."[10]

2
Edwards' Concept of Sin

Supporting Edwards' vision of hell was a concept of sin that he articulated throughout his writings but brought to a final and definitive statement in *The Great Christian Doctrine of Original Sin,* published in 1758, the year of his death. Although intended as an ostensible and specific answer to the Rev. John Taylor's *Scripture-Doctrine of Original Sin* (1738), and to a lesser extent to the Rev. George Turnbull's *The Principles of Moral Philosophy* (1740) and *Christian Philosophy* (1740), Edwards' treatise took as its larger target the whole rising tide of liberalism. His interpretation of sin grew from the conviction that all human nature is fundamentally alienated from God. This condition, Edwards wrote, "is *inherent,* and is seated in that *nature* which is common to all mankind."[11] For a brief time Adam had lived in harmony with God; but when Adam sinned his divine nature was withdrawn and he was left standing alone, superior in intelligence to brute animals but nevertheless separated from the source of spiritual life and light. In opposition to the Arminian interpretation, founded upon Pelagius' argument that Adam's sin was his alone and that it in no way affected his posterity,[12] Edwards held that as children of Adam we are all sinners by origin. Adam's sin was not his alone but "is seated" in that nature common to all. Because, according to Edwards, every man shares this common nature, he has, as it were, committed Adam's sin. This is true of persons "of all constitutions, capacities, nations and ages" (*Original Sin*, 124).

Given this universal condition, human beings may be said to manifest a fixed direction towards sin, an inclination of the heart that precedes all volition and all action. Regardless of their "thousands" and "millions" of good works, all men share this "unfailing propensity" to moral evil (*OS*, 128). The basis has to do with "motive." In Edwards' massive *Freedom of the Will*, published four years earlier in 1754, he said that prior to will, by which the mind voluntarily chooses either one thing or another, there is a more fundamental cause identified as motive.[13] By this term he meant "the *whole* of that which moves, excites or invites the mind to volition."[14] A person is free to do what he wills; he enjoys freedom in the exercise of this liberty. But will, which is not its own cause, is determined by something outside and beyond itself. In *Original Sin* Edwards uses the terms "propensity" and "tendency" to express this same idea, and in *Religious Affections,* the term "inclination." The rationale welding these terms together makes clear that volitional acts have causes rooted in a common and determined human disposition. According to Clarence H. Faust, Edwards' unequivocal answer to the question "With what dispositions do men come into the world?" was based upon his argument against the freedom of the will. He affirmed "uncompromisingly," said Faust, "the Calvinistic belief that men enter this life totally depraved—enter it with dispositions that made them wholly unable of themselves either to do good or to avoid evil."[15] The capstone of Edwards' argument appeared in *The Nature of True Virtue* (posthumously, 1765), in which he identified this disposition once and for all as that of self-love.[16] With man's nature determined and fixed towards self, not towards God, the subsequent logic looms clearly: "According as a man is inclined, so he perceives; as he perceives, so he chooses; as he chooses, so he acts."[17]

To be disposed inflexibly towards self-love is both an inherent quality of human nature and the essence of its depravity. As Edwards declared in a 1740 sermon, the natural love of self presupposes an enmity against God, inclining the heart to shun God's presence as well as His infinitude ("Hypocrites Deficient in Prayer,"

II,73). Self-love glorifies the creature instead of the Creator. It declares its "ontological independence"; it equates the circumference of human existence with "the perimeter of Being-itself." [18] This is man's grand illusion. This is his awesome depravity.

In short, man's natural inclination is towards independence, a state of being out of relationship with God, or, more exactly, of not being in Christ ("Justification by Faith Alone," I,629). Contrary to Christian freedom, which obtains only in "closing with Christ," the grand illusion posits freedom as independent of grace, and virtue as identical with self-love. The truth of the matter, according to Edwards, is that instead of illuminating human existence self-love darkens the mind and hardens the heart. It silences the conscience, perverts religion, and alienates man from the source of all love and grace. What self-love regards as the power of light is instead the power of blackness. And instead of light the heart is itself a dungeon. In man's inherent failure to relish divine things, to consent to true Being, to close with Christ, the human heart is corrupted by its own pride.

To make the reader truly sensible of sin in this treatise on original sin, Edwards used the image of "death." Notions about inherent and universal depravity; about man's fixed propensity to sin; about the "odious," "detestable," "pernicious," and "destructive" quality of this propensity, all take as a common denominator "the universal reign of *death*" (*OS*,129,206). For Edwards it doubly signified not only the cessation of life but also the state of one's being outside of Christ. It is the state of "perfect misery, and sensible destruction . . . the loss of that holy principle, which was in the highest sense the life of the soul." In this condition—"truly ruined and undone . . . corrupt, miserable and helpless"—a person "is dead" (*OS*,243,258-259).

With commanding authority Edwards spoke out relentlessly on this subject. His task, however, was always something more than to expound abstract ideas, which would remain barren unless he quickened his hearers to a consciousness of sin. It was precisely here that the greater challenge presented itself to Edwards. For not only did he regard the unregenerate as spiritually dead, but to him their sin was compounded by the fact that they were blind to their own condition. Sin was "first and foremost a blindness"—and only afterwards a perversity whereby natural man sees "the great as little, the beautiful as negligible, the holy as undesirable, the glorious as a dull and despicable thing."[19] In all this he sees nothing of his real self. Edwards' task was to guide his listeners into self-consciousness, to take them on a perilous journey into themselves.

The difficulty was always to have them confront themselves as they were. Evidence abounded to assure them of their goodness. Edwards himself recognized that natural men are capable of and, indeed, do perform many ethically good deeds. Northampton had its share of good citizens and neighbors. Even Calvin had celebrated the great gifts of intelligence and imagination that God had bestowed upon human nature. There was no question that, endowed with a longing for truth, people displayed impressive achievements in the sciences, the arts, philosophy, and law. Calvin recognized that those whom Scripture calls "natural men" were, indeed, "sharp and penetrating." "Let us," he adjured, "learn by their example how many gifts the Lord left to human nature even after it was despoiled of its true good."[20] As if these concessions to natural goodness were not enough, Calvin went further to suggest a "natural instinct, an awareness of divinity . . . a sense of deity inscribed in the hearts of all." This condition, he said, was "beyond controversy."[21]

Nevertheless, there was also the incontrovertible fact of sin. It might be said that in the idea of "nevertheless" the real significance of the Reformation lies. The radical discontinuity which the term implies was the same that broke the medieval synthesis of nature and grace, reason and revelation.[22] The point concerning Edwards is exactly the one that infuses his writing, as it did Calvin's. Regardless of all reasonable evidence to the contrary, nature is nevertheless determined towards evil and is totally corrupt. Edwards asserted that the blindness unto sin is not the fault of man's natural faculties: "God has given men faculties truly noble and excellent"; nor is the blindness "like the ignorance of a new-born infant" ("Man's Natural Blindness in the Things of Religion," II,247). The blindness is rather from some "positive cause" that Edwards identified as "a principle" in the human heart that hinders the faculties in religious matters (II,247). This being the case, Edwards urged the good citizens and neighbors of Northampton to wake up to themselves: "search your own heart" ("Men Naturally are God's Enemies," II,134). His words echoed those beginning Calvin's *Institutes*—"Without knowledge of self there is no knowledge of God"[23] —as well as those spoken by sages and prophets centuries before. To Edwards the imperative "Know thyself" meant, look beneath your "goodness," search the old wounds to the bottom so that they can be healed. Without this inward search, without acknowledging inherent sin, any healing that supposedly takes place is vain and deceitful. Edwards declared to all Northampton that though they seem to live in peace, there is no peace outside of Christ's radical grace.

The fact remained for Edwards that sinners had no such insight. They could neither rejoice in God's holiness nor shudder at their alienation from God. Their complacent conscience insulated them from all that is mysterious. Edwards' demand for wakefulness resembles Rudolf Otto's assertion that if man could only shudder he would know what having the fear of God means. For "shuddering," Otto said, "is something more than 'natural,' ordinary fear . . . it implies that the mysterious is already beginning to loom before the mind, to touch the feeling."[24] Natural man is destitute of such a "sense." Even though he may be conscious of having committed harmful acts or of being in discord with his neighbor and himself, he knows nothing of himself as sinner, and sin and salvation are only so many tedious arguments. This self-blindness is what Edwards sought to shatter. He believed that natural man, alienated from God, recognizes himself only when confronted by God in Christ.[25] Unless he enters into "the spirit," he knows nothing of his true status, even though he may rightly see himself as sincere, self-disciplined, resourceful, morally energetic, and careful in business. It was to such an upstanding citizen that Edwards preached about sin.

Before looking at the way Edwards aroused New England's torpid conscience and forced people to gape into the hell of their real condition, we need to reiterate that in Edwards' concept of sin alienation presupposed a blindness to it. The Reformers had known that natural man, deluded by self-sufficiency, had no sense of hell, no sense of alienation from God.[26] Like the Reformers, Edwards knew that self-sufficiency, fostered by liberal theology, protected the unregenerate from sensing the depths of sin and the power of evil that had been at "the center of Luther's experience as it was in

Paul's."[27] What Edwards knew better than any of his eighteenth-century contemporaries was that original sin was profoundly true of all men, past and present. In his preaching about hell, he sought to make his listeners conscious of it at their present moment—to awaken them to themselves, to have them apprehend hell as separation from God, and to expose them to their own delusions, blindness, and death.

On the abstract level he said that man's insensibility stems from a natural "principle of atheism," a refusal to recognize divine Beingness ("Men Naturally Are God's Enemies," II,134). Elsewhere he described this spirit of atheism as a type of understanding that is "full of darkness" and of a mind that is "blind to spiritual things" ("Natural Men in a Dreadful Condition," II,817). On the level of everyday experience Edwards interpreted insensibility first as self-sufficiency, pride, smugness—and, secondly, as the apathy that leaves one's soul, like that of T. S. Eliot's Prufrock, etherized, unaware of life's contingencies, benumbed to one's own insecurity and to the danger "of dropping into hell before to-morrow morning" ("Natural Men. . . ," II,823). Edwards' message burned into the core of present existence. With false securities fractured, it called for the perilous quest into the self where foundations are shaken and men shudder.

Underlying Edwards' hellfire sermons is the Calvinist insistence that self-knowledge comes first. Unless persons first see their splintered selves, they remain outside the saving knowledge of divine things. To see hellfire and to shudder begins the drama of salvation. But first Edwards had to make his audience mindful of their natural apathy.[28] Of the sermons written to do precisely this, the most effective is "Man's Natural Blindness in the Things of Religion." The theme concerns the deceitful ways by which persons avert their eyes from painful self-examination. Edwards' analysis builds to a crescendo:

> What can be more plain in itself, than that eternal things are of infinitely greater importance than temporal things? And yet how hard is it thoroughly to convince men of it! How plain is it, that eternal misery in hell is infinitely to be dreaded! And yet how few appear to be thoroughly convinced of this! How plain is it, that life is uncertain! And yet how much otherwise do most men think! . . . There is no one thing whatsoever more plain and manifest, and more demonstrable, than the being of God. It is manifest in ourselves, in our bodies and souls, and in everything about us

wherever we turn our eye, whether to heaven, or to earth, the air, or the
seas. And yet how prone is the heart of man to call this into question!
(II,252)

What Edwards called into question were the foolish things of this
world, the state of "good men," the wisdom that rests upon human
learning. Only revelation illumines the darkness in which fools live,
and only such light brings true wisdom. But to obtain this sovereign
gift of God, Edwards demanded the prior recognition of weakness,
blindness, and misery. "True wisdom," he said, "is a precious jewel"
(II,256), bought at a great and painful price.

Troubling Edwards was the fact that in settling for theological
liberalism New Englanders were being satisfied with too little. What
R. W. B. Lewis in *The American Adam* calls a "lack of richness"
characterized liberalism, which in abandoning a sense of sin had
transformed the human drama into something Edwards regarded as
flat, colorless, and boring. More importantly, it had expunged suffering, to say nothing of terror, from the way of salvation. It had
nullified the Pauline paradox "Where sin abounded, grace did much
more abound" (Romans 5:20), and had silenced the question that
Nathaniel Hawthorne, echoing Edwards, asked a hundred years later
in *The Marble Faun:* "Is sin, then,—which we deem such a dreadful
blackness in the universe,—is it, like sorrow, merely an element of
human education through which we struggle to a higher and purer
state than we could otherwise have attained?" (ch. 50). It was the
grandeur of this question that Arminianism failed to grasp, and that
Edwards understood full well when he wrote:

> There would be no manifestation of God's grace or true goodness, if there
> was no sin to be pardoned, no misery to be saved from.... We little
> consider how much the sense of good is heightened by the sense of evil,
> both moral and natural. And it is necessary that there should be evil,
> because the display of the glory of God could not but be imperfect and
> incomplete without it, so evil is necessary, in order to the highest happiness
> of the creature, and the completeness of that communication of God, for
> which he made the world ... for, as we have said, the sense of good is
> comparatively dull and flat, without the knowledge of evil. ("Concerning
> the Divine Decrees in General, and Election in Particular," II,528)

For Edwards the knowledge of evil meant concomitant suffering:
knowledge and experience were always one and the same. It was

knowledge in this full sense that Edwards wanted his imprecatory sermons to convey—knowledge that would lead people to repentance. In the total view Edwards did not regard suffering as a penalty for sin but as a correction against future sin. Sin was its own punishment, terror, and misery. Calvin had emphasized the same point by quoting Augustine: " 'What you suffer, what you complain about, is your medicine, not your penalty; your chastisement, not your condemnation. . . . Know, brethren, that all this misery of humankind in which the world groans is medicinal pain and not a penal sentence.' "[29]

The important point is that sin makes salvation meaningful. To experience and preach salvation presupposes sin, just as light presupposes darkness. Only through the knowledge of evil, Edwards said, will the completeness and true goodness of God's grace be manifested. Towards this certainty Edwards directed his hellfire sermons.

3
Hell as Vision and Image

When we remember that Edwards preached of hell to so-called natural or unregenerate men, who themselves had no such vision, we recognize at once the suitability of his imagery. For example, the metaphor of the spider: "The God that holds you over the pit of hell, much as one holds a spider, or some loathsome insect over the fire, abhors you, and is dreadfully provoked" ("Sinners in the Hands of an Angry God," II,10). Man, with his propensity towards self-love, is "naturally" God's enemy. Instead of closing with God through Christ, he exists apart, as dangerously near to nonbeing as a spider dangling over the rising flames. The image reveals Edwards' concern not for the condition of spiders or even of man but for the relation between sinful man and God. It is at best a precarious relation, kept intact only by the mercy of God, but subject also to His arbitrary judgment and dissolution. The image carries essential metaphysical meaning. But for the slender thread, unredeemed and finite man is lost forever in the abyss of dissolution. Edwards here is using language that represents spiritual truth through the particular image and at the same time requires a sanctified eye to discern the analogy. The suitability of the spider image is in the truth that is revealed to sanctified vision. Being in the Spirit, a person can discern the condition of sinful man who is outside the Spirit.

The imagery is suitable for other reasons. Edwards thought of words and ideas as being in mutual assimilation. Instead of arbitrary counters, words as actual ideas are something to be felt, sensed, and experienced. Figurative language places ideas in the mind, and thus the word becomes the event. Apart from the theory that words arouse sensation, the more important point is that words become the idea, and thus the purity of language rests in the fact that through transparent language ideas are suddenly apprehended. Nothing comes between the language-event and the apprehension-event, between the physical image of the spider and the sense of sin. Thus, like an eighteenth-century Kafka, Edwards shocked his hearers out of their "irrelevant and fruitless Sunday musings"[30] and, even more importantly, forced them to confront their woeful condition in the very image.

By means of imagery that springs from religious rather than aesthetic vision, Edwards sought to effect a threefold strategy. The *first phase* was to awaken people to their natural condition. That this condition consisted of pride, enmity, contempt, atheism, blasphemy became sensible knowledge to them when, transfixing them with his eye, Edwards spoke of "a little, wretched, despicable creature; a worm, a mere nothing, and less than nothing; a vile insect, that has risen up in contempt against the Majesty of heaven and earth" ("The Justice of God in the Damnation of Sinners," I,673). Edwards intensified his listeners' consciousness by depicting this creature engulfed in destruction. He then proceeded to drop the vile insect into the pit. His image is utterly of this world: "You have often seen a spider, or some other noisome insect, when thrown into the midst of a fierce fire, and have observed how immediately it yields to the force of the flames. . . . Here is a little image of what you will be in hell, except you repent and fly to Christ" ("The Future Punishment of the Wicked Unavoidable and Intolerable," II,82). Edwards equated annihilation with spiritual death, with what he called "dying in the highest sense of the word." With great insight he said that this kind of dying was

> to die sensibly; to die and know it; to be sensible of the gloom of death.
> This is to be undone; this is worthy of the name of destruction. This
> sinking of the soul under an infinite weight, which it cannot bear, is the
> gloom of hell. We read in Scripture of blackness of darkness; this is it, this
> is the very thing. (II,81)

This is the death revealed by the law and spoken of by Paul (Romans
3:9-20). Not until the sense of sin fills our consciousness are we
prepared to hear the saving gospel. That this death had undone so
many, that hell was the state of death in which the unconverted
"lived," that if they were to speak their true voice they would
"shake and tremble, and cry out, and shriek, and gnash [their]
teeth" (II,82)—these were the truths made sensible through Edwards' images of spiders, flames, and death. Nothing less than a
terrifying sense could measure their metaphysical importance.

The *second phase* required the kind of language that would
convince sinners of God's justice in their condemnation, give them a
willingness to be damned, and make them accept the hell they
deserved. Edwards' logic in this matter, most effectively put forth in
"The Justice of God in the Damnation of Sinners," presupposed a
universe founded upon what he called a "mutual answerableness"
between the way God deals with man and man's own actions
(I,672). Accordingly, every sin deserves punishment. If there is
anyone whom we are "under infinite obligations" to love, honor,
and obey, then contrary behavior towards that person must be
"infinitely faulty" (I,669). If that object is God, and if He is
infinitely loving and has infinite excellency and beauty, then sin
against God is infinitely heinous and demands infinite punishment.
Edwards strove to convince hearers of this fact by depicting an angry
and wrathful God whose judgments are "strict, exact, awful, and
terrible, and therefore glorious" ("The Eternity of Hell Torments,"
II,87). To convince them that the "hands of an angry God" are also
the "hands of a great God" ("The Future Punishment. . . ," II,82),
Edwards exposed his congregation to that wrath. In characteristic
prose he wrote:

> The wrath of a king is the roaring of a lion; but this is the wrath of
> Jehovah, the Lord God Omnipotent. . . . What must be the uttermost of his
> wrath, who made heaven and earth by the word of his power; who spake,
> and it was done, who commanded, and it stood fast! What must his wrath
> be, who commandeth the sun, and it rises not, and sealeth up the stars!

> What must his wrath be, who shaketh the earth out of its place, and causeth the pillars of heaven to tremble! What must his wrath be, who rebuketh the sea, and maketh it dry, who removeth the mountains out of their places, and overturneth them in his anger! What must his wrath be, whose majesty is so awful, that no man could live in the sight of it! ("When the Wicked Shall Have Filled Up the Measure of Their Sin," II,124)

Edwards spared no effort to convince his hearers that sin brings consequences in a moral universe. In a manuscript entitled "Directions for Judging of Persons' Experiences," consisting of criteria by which to determine the authenticity of religious experience, he insisted that fellow ministers "see to it" that their congregations have a true conviction that damnation is the just consequence of their sinfulness, and, furthermore, that their experiences of God's justice "are not superficial pangs, flashes, imagination, freaks, but solid, substantial, deep, inwrought into the frame and temper of their minds."[31] Edwards would have his sermons implant this conviction into the consciousness of New Englanders.

This interpretation of Edwards' preaching must not blur the distinction between hell as separation from God (*poena damni*) and hell as punishment by God (*poena sensus*). Even though Edwards' imagery suggests the latter, he avoided the fatal dichotomy between God as just and angry, and Christ as merciful and loving, as well as the bizarre representation of God as loving and angry by turns. In Edwards' view the supreme attributes of God have to do with excellency and beauty; His severity is encompassed by gloriousness, and His judgments by love. We are not to forget that whereas love and hate are contradictory, love and wrath are not. All too often interpreters have depicted Edwards, himself supposedly subject to alternating moods, as an erratic evangelist who projected inconsistencies upon God. Moreover, they have interpreted his hellfire imagery literally, as if the God envisioned by Edwards were a sadist who enjoyed tormenting humankind. The divine wrath that Edwards depicted belongs in the end to the sphere of law, curse, sin, and death—to man's state of alienation from God and not to God's own affections. His thoroughly Biblical imagery was rooted in Calvinist theology. Calvin had said that because descriptions can never deal adequately with God's justice, it must be "figuratively expressed to us by physical things." Persons must be made to "*feel* heaven, earth, living beings, and all that exists aflame, as it were, with dire anger against them, and armed to destroy them."[32] What end does such imagery serve? Like Edwards, Calvin called for imagery of fire and brimstone to describe the hell of separation, of "how wretched it is to be cut off from all fellowship with God."[33] Edwards' descriptions of a God of wrath and anger force sensible recognition not of God's emotions but of the cosmic consequences of sin working themselves out through the whole of creation, which in Paul's language "groaneth and travaileth in pain" (Romans 6:22).

Language initially intended to awaken natural men to their sinfulness and then to convince them of God's justice in their condemnation served a *third phase,* namely, to prepare them to hear the gospel. Awful apprehensions of spiders, lakes of fire, blackness, bottomless pits, and divine wrath made way for the assurance that "God offers you a Savior" ("The Justice of God. . . ," II,674). This gift of all-sufficient grace would be meaningless, however, unless men were first made sensible of their guilt and their deserved punishment. It was impossible, Edwards argued, that a person who is not first convinced of his guilt would be willing to accept the offer of an atonement. Edwards' logic not only made good theology; it was also sound rhetoric and psychology. For if one has not known sin and its consequences, or "if you have not really deserved everlasting burnings in hell" (II,675), the very offer is a repugnant imposition. Edwards made certain that his listeners were left panting for cool water. One of the reasons his sermon "The Justice of God in the Damnation of Sinners" is exemplary of his best imprecatory preaching is that in this sermon all three phases are handled with consummate effect.[34] The hell is nowhere hotter—and the saving assurance is nowhere more satisfying: "I would conclude this discourse by putting the godly in mind of the freeness and wonderfulness of the grace of God towards them" (II,679). A similar conclusion illumines the gloom of his sermon "The End of the Wicked Contemplated": "If you repent before it is too late, you yourselves shall be of that joyful company . . . and you will enter into the joy of your Lord, and there shall never be any end or abatement of your joy!" (II,212).

But whereas his sermon "The Justice of God . . . " is the more satisfactory example of Edwards' hellfire preaching, it is his sermon preached at Enfield, Connecticut—"Sinners in the Hands of an Angry God"—by which later generations came to know Jonathan Edwards. No other sermon preached in America has received comparable attention.

4
"Sinners in the Hands of an Angry God"

To put this amazing sermon into an *American* perspective, Paul Elmer More, the unswerving humanist of the 1920's, can serve as a starting point. As a literary critic he realized that something awesome infused Edwards' language. He went on to praise Edwards' "sincerity of vision," but he never ventured further.[35] He approached Edwards' Calvinist world only closely enough to note, quoting Edwards' early biographer Alexander V. G. Allen, that here was a man almost too great "to let loose upon other men in their ordinary condition."[36] Edwards was like "some organ of vast capacity whose strongest stops or combinations should never have been drawn."[37] This assessment that the American Calvinist was "let loose" upon his Northampton congregation for over twenty years hardly describes his ministry, characterized by unstinting love and concern for the welfare of his parishioners. Yet it is true these same parishioners discharged Edwards, and one supposes that when he left Northampton for good in 1751, the townspeople sighed in relief. From Edwards' day to More's, persons who gazed into the hell depicted by Edwards quickly stepped back when the shock disturbed their ordinary and well-ordered lives.[38]

Of course Edwards was preaching an increasingly unacceptable Calvinism that allowed no ameliorating compromises between God and man, and between natural and regenerate man. He refused to bend his orthodoxy to accommodate New Englanders who in growing numbers demanded from their clergy assurance that God favored morality at least as much as piety; who saw no reason why the unregenerate should be denied the sacrament of communion, especially since Edwards' own grandfather and predecessor, Solomon

Stoddard, had held that communion itself could prove a regenerative experience; and who demanded that church membership include even those persons unwilling or unable to profess prior religious experience. That Edwards opposed the liberals on every front did not prevent progressive enlightenment from winning the day.

To what extent, however, did Edwards' ostracism result from theological disputes alone? Granting their importance, plus the significance of the niggling personal circumstances that biographer Ola Winslow associates with his dismissal,[39] all this nevertheless fails to explain the peculiar vehemence among his detractors. What is even more intriguing is that this feeling never really subsided. A century after Edwards' death Oliver Wendell Holmes, with patronizing restraint, revealed deep hostility to a theology rooted in "the deepest depths of hell" and to language which "shocks the sensibilities of a later generation."[40] Had Edwards lived longer, Holmes mused, "I have no doubt his creed would have softened into a kindly, humanized belief."[41] With such good fortune, Edwards supposedly would have realized that civilization had outgrown what to Holmes was the detestable myth of the Fall and "the legendary Inferno." Moreover, he would have learned the lesson that hell "is not much talked about nowadays to ears polite or impolite"—that, in fact, "humanity is shocked and repelled by it."[42] At the turn of the century, William James, putting his avowed objectivity aside, took up the same criticism by saying that "to-day we abhor" Edwards' doctrine of hell and salvation, which "appears to us, if sovereignly anything, sovereignly irrational and mean."[43] Less restrained scorn produced all manner of caricature, the most outrageous being that of Clarence Darrow, who wrote in H. L. Mencken's *American Mercury* that Edwards' "main business in the world was scaring silly women and little children and blaspheming the God he professed to adore." Not satisfied with this broadside, he added: "Nothing but a distorted or diseased mind could have produced his 'Sinners in the Hands of an Angry God.' "[44] Still another detractor, Vernon Louis Parrington, tried to explain what he considered the tragedy of Edwards' intellectual life, namely, that theology had triumphed over philosophy. Edwards, he thought, would have become a strikingly creative thinker had not his religious conversion unfortunately "interrupted" him. Then, with scarcely hidden derision, Parrington conjectured that we really do not regret that Edwards stoked the fires of hell. For "once the horrors that lay in the background of Calvinism were disclosed to common view, the system was doomed."[45]

It was not Edwards' theology alone that provoked this antagonism. What was "let loose" upon New England worshipers, including those at Enfield, and what continued to unsettle later generations was a vision matching that of the greatest poets and prophets, whose implicit mission has always been to shock. Plato in *The Republic* knew that poets were dangerous, just as Dostoevsky's Grand Inquisitor in *The Brothers Karamazov* realized that prophets must be silenced. Both kinds of men were an offense to the common person living within his familiar world. Edwards' public downfall, if it can be called such, was his having dared to envision heaven and hell and then to speak of that vision in language which most persons could not endure. He expected his people to feel with full heart the tensions he created. During the brief Awakening, these same listeners managed to sustain such feelings, as well as to learn the difference between morality and conversion, good works and religious affections, self-sufficiency and irresistible grace. But when sustained interminably, such tensions induce the state of dread Kierkegaard described under the category of consciousness. The more we are conscious of both finitude and infinitude, the greater the dread. "The greater the dread, the greater the man," Kierkegaard added.[46] To be called to this kind of greatness is hardly anyone's desire, and it definitely was not the desire of Edwards' congregation. People needed nearer things to think about. Yet, with an irony that would have puzzled even Edwards, his "Sinners in the Hands of an Angry God," for all the apocalyptic dread it induced and for all its irrelevance to the American Dream, became the most famous sermon ever preached in the land.

To identify the sermon as the culmination of the Great Awakening further clarifies the American perspective. Religious revivalism, which had spread up and down the Connecticut Valley in the 1730's, had reached a high pitch throughout New England by the time Edwards preached to the Enfield congregation on July 8, 1741. Marvelous things had already happened among his own Northampton people several years earlier, described in Edwards' letter (May 30, 1735) to the Rev. Benjamin Colman of Boston's Brattle Street

Church. Even though there is no evidence that Colman ever had this letter published, the happenings in Northampton were of such importance that Edwards later enlarged this account and published it in 1737 as *A Faithful Narrative of the Surprising Work of God in the Conversion of Many Hundred Souls in Northampton, and in Neighboring Towns and Villages,* a work that opened the avenue "into emotion and sensibility."[47] This, of course, is what the Great Awakening was all about. As a sudden alternative to genteel rationalism, it made religious enthusiasm something public and democratic. Furthermore, in a way Edwards could never have foretold, it inspired a wholly new American temper—anti-authority, anti-aristocratic, anti-Eastern, anti-theological—which Richard Hofstadter has identified as American anti-intellectualism.[48]

Edwards, however, also considered these public revivals as profoundly personal experiences for individuals—a transforming, regenerative experience touching the deepest levels of being and opening the heart to a sense of divine reality. Although disturbed over public excesses and subsequent criticism, he indefatigably preached the sense of the heart, and made this sense theologically understandable in such works as *The Distinguishing Marks of a Work of the Spirit of God* and *Some Thoughts Concerning the Present Revival in New England.* These two books laid the groundwork for *A Treatise Concerning Religious Affections.*

When "Sinners in the Hands of an Angry God" is read within the context of the Great Awakening and Edwards' own deepening search for the meaning of religious experience, its importance far surpasses the popular judgment of those persons who regard it only as hellfire. To digress briefly, it is noteworthy that certain apologists, as if embarrassed by Edwards' fire and brimstone, insist he was not this kind of preacher. "When he was most himself," Ola Winslow writes, "he was a quiet-spoken teacher."[49] Douglas J. Elwood asserts that "Sinners in the Hands of an Angry God" is more representative of Edwards' times than of the man.[50] Still another student of Edwards, Thomas A. Johnson, minimizes this side of Edwards by claiming that only about one-third of all his sermons were disciplinary (*i.e.,* imprecatory, corrective, hortatory). By far the greater number consisted of pastoral sermons that set forth "in positive, joyous, tender, rhapsodic, and even rapt language the beauty of religious contemplation."[51]   Finally, we might notice that whereas Edwards based his fiery Enfield sermon upon the scriptural text from Deuteronomy 32:35—"Their feet shall slide in due time"—he wrote in far different tones about another text from the same chapter (32:2). About this text—"My doctrine shall drop as the rain; my speech shall distil as the dew, as the small rain upon the tender herb, and as showers upon the grass"—Edwards observed:

> God here speaks to the people quite in a different manner from what he did at Mount Sinai, when he spake to them out of the midst of the fire. God's word then was like thunder and lightning and devouring fire, threatening to overbear and consume so frail and tender a creature as man, who is like the grass and flower of the field. It is heard in pleasant song. Instead of being like lightning to destroy and consume, it is like the gentle showers, and refreshing dew on the tender grass, revealing, not his wrath, but his great mercy, in a manner adapted to men's tender frame. In this song is much of the glorious gospel.[52]

Calling attention to this other side of Edwards' preaching quickly dispels the distorted popular impression that hellfire blazed in all Edwards' sermons.

However, we return to the point: Edwards emphatically did preach hell in imagistic terms of spiders suspended on threads over devouring flames. While it is true, as his apologists point out, that this is not all he preached; that his sermons on salvation rose as lyrically high as those on sin plumbed the depths; that pastoral sermons outnumbered disciplinary ones—yet, as Peter Gay correctly says,

> to minimize the importance, and explain away the doctrine, of the Enfield sermon is to do Edwards a dubious favor; it is to make him inoffensive by emasculating him. Edwards did not want to be inoffensive. God was omnipotent, God was angry, man was wholly lost without God: these were the pillars sustaining the structure of Edwards' theology.[53]

It is essential, therefore, to recognize Edwards' vision of hell for what it is. This is *not* to say that Holmes, Darrow, and Parrington—to name but three of the more severe detractors—recognized anything important.[54]   Nor is it to suggest that Edwards himself abandoned intellectual severity for what to the George Whitefields of his day became evangelical emotionalism. And certainly it is not to argue that Edwards wished to establish the kind of religious fundamentalism that later swept western America. The essential point is that to Edwards hell is inseparable from religious experience. To know salvation is first to know the dark night of alienation.

Such a moment as Edwards presents in "Sinners in the Hands of an Angry God" corresponds with the dreadful consciousness that an all-sovereign God has destroyed all human deceits, has laid bare all secret motives, and has shattered all confidence in human strength, achievements, prudence, and contrivances. Security known in good health, in well-laid schemes, and even in a Covenant Theology becomes nothing. Whether one chooses the image of a spider's thread or the thinnest layer of cortex to describe insecurity, only God's arbitrary will keeps one from annihilation. Were we to visit death's kingdom, Edwards said in this sermon, and inquire about the lost ones, "we doubtless should hear one and another reply, 'No, I never intended to come here: I had lived out matters otherwise in my mind; I thought I should contrive well for myself: I thought my scheme good . . . and when I was saying, Peace and safety, then sudden destruction came upon me' " (II,9). This destructive moment that strips away all illusion is the same overpowering and numinous moment when we see into the heart of darkness, there to discover, as Martin Luther wrote, that God, "more terrible and frightful than the Devil . . . dealeth with us and bringeth us to ruin with power, smiteth and hammereth us and payeth no heed to us. . . . In His majesty He is a consuming fire."[55]

The truly audacious feature of the sermon is the way Edwards presented the cosmic proportions of this moment. His imagery appropriates the basic elements of *air, earth, fire,* and *water,* all conspiring in man's destruction. God's enemies are mere chaff before the "whirlwind," and their destruction will come "like a whirlwind" (II,8,9). Except for the sovereign will of God, the "earth would not bear [them] one moment," and their security is no more than that of a spider's web "to stop a falling rock" (II,9). Furthermore, "flames gather and flash around them" (II,9). The water too is rising to burst the dam, and "there is nothing but the mere pleasure of God, that holds the waters back" (II,9). This typological imagery does more than excite sensible experience; it relates all creation to the concrete and present world. But in positioning man amid the natural elements, it also suggests his aloneness in the vastness of time and space. His hell will be "long ages, millions of millions of ages," just as even now he exists suspended in space with "nothing to stand upon nor any thing to take hold of" (II,11,9). What this cosmic imagery unfolds with frightening relevance is the utter inconsequence of man's pride and free will, his total alienation from the source of life, and a transcendent God who is under no obligation to man's self-interests.

To miss the contemporaneity of this sermon corroborates Berdyaev's verdict that smugness today may indeed have an eschatological character and "may be man's final destiny."[56] To dispel the smugness of his own day, Edwards reinforced the visionary and verbal power of "Sinners in the Hands of an Angry God" by the straightforward statement beginning the "Application" section of the sermon. "The use of this awful subject," he said, "may be for awakening unconverted persons in this congregation" (II,9). But the terror imparted by "this awful subject" has proved to be something more than that associated with Enfield and the short-lived Awakening. The terror is also that of modern man's insecurity. In this sermon Edwards brings mankind, "without mitigation, protection, or indulgence," face to face with a universe devoid of security or refuge. "Sinners in the Hands of an Angry God" can thus be called, to use Perry Miller's expression, America's "sudden leap into modernity."[57] The sermon represents, as H. Richard Niebuhr has said about Edwards' preaching, a religious awareness that men at every moment are "as ready to plunge into the abyss of disintegration, barbarism, crime and war of all against all, as to advance toward harmony and integration." According to Niebuhr, Edwards recognized "what Kierkegaard meant when he described life as treading water with ten thousand fathoms beneath us."[58] It is not putting the case too strongly to say with James Carse that Edwards' sermons, particularly "Sinners in the Hands of an Angry God," "were for his time what Picasso's 'Guernica' is for ours."[59]

No modern mind has understood this condition better than Kierkegaard. That Edwards' sermon has proved an offense to subsequent generations of readers bears exactly upon the point Kierkegaard stressed regarding the offensiveness of Christianity itself. Both thinkers affirmed that Christianity begins with the doctrine of sin. This doctrine establishes at once the category of the individual as opposed to the category of the universal. The offense is that a particular individual should have such a reality and, moreover, that his sin should concern God. The offense is that Christianity requires the singular person to be himself before God and not to stand in abstract relationship to the universal Good, the Beautiful, and the True, whether through intellect or imagination. Indeed the offense is the thread-like relationship itself between the singular man and the all-sovereign God. Once more, the offense, Kierkegaard said, is not that Christianity is so dark, so gloomy, so severe, but rather that "it would make of man something so extraordinary that he is unable to get it into his head."[60]

In dramatizing the consequences of the broken thread, Edwards compounded the awe. Air, earth, fire, and water are all seen to represent instruments bringing about man's destruction. His separation is total and his death eternal. Having willed to reject the man-God relationship and to consent only to his own human excellence, having turned away from the offense and its saving power, the sinner, no longer in God's hands, is forever lost. "Sinners in the Hands of an Angry God" demonstrates the vision Edwards brought to this side of religious experience. He saw into the condition of persons willfully living apart from God. In language that seems to rest in the vision, as if accidental to it, Edwards preached of this hell in order that his listeners might be prepared to envision with him the heaven promised by the saving gospel.

CHAPTER SIX

Salvation

1
Prelude

Even though Edwards induced all manner of fright among his New England people, he never intended his great hellfire sermons to be anything other than a prelude to a far more important subject. To be sure, hell was a necessary prelude. He never doubted the importance of one's gaining a conviction of sin. But it was a conviction, a self-knowledge, intended to render one capable of the joy of salvation, always Edwards' greater subject.

This insistence has an important bearing upon Edwards and the subject of tragedy. Upheld by the Pauline faith that the gospel has replaced the law, Edwards' religious vision extended beyond tragedy. Some writers have argued, on the contrary, that Puritanism held to a tragic vision based on what William E. Rowley called "the essential tragedy of the fall of man."[1] Concerning Edwards specifically, Robert Spiller calls his philosophical system a "house of tragedy in which the sense of guilt and agony survives" and the release into the "peace of submission" fails. It was, Spiller says, a structure of tragic realization "repeated in the work of Poe, Hawthorne, and Melville; O'Neill, Eliot, and Faulkner."[2] The trouble with this interpretation is that it stops short of Edwards' vision of salvation. Of those writers in Spiller's list only T. S. Eliot knew this vision, if, indeed, the multifoliate rose in his *Four Quartets* symbolizes the soteriological vision. As for Edwards, there is a progressive enlargement of spirit that Alan Heimert correctly calls "the millennial vision," and that Elwood heralds as Edwards' "cosmic optimism."[3] Following the notion that at the heart of Puritanism was an "indestructible optimism,"[4] both Heimert and Elwood assert convincingly that in the last analysis all cataclysm and all evil, identified as being within the circle of finitude, are themselves encircled by the infinite reality of God. This is to claim, with Edwards, that all tragic dislocations are resolved within the larger context. The tragedy of Everyman loses its sting and finally its status within the all-encompassing excellency and saving love of God.

2
Grace and Personal Salvation

Edwards spoke about the ultimate terms of salvation. First of all, his basic premise was the same that undergirded orthodox theology, namely, "an omnipotent God and an impotent man."[5] With the greatest humility we must adore "the awful and absolute sovereignty of God," and only to His "sovereign grace" can we attribute our salvation ("God's Sovereignty in the Salvation of Man," II,853,854). On this premise Edwards then declared salvation to be that divine power which resolves sin and rescues man from all other problems that torment him. Edwards' goal, like that of his Calvinist forebears, was salvation—the ultimate deliverance from the demonic power of evil, sin, and death. Justification *sola fide* was the acquittal of sin; salvation was the new freedom from sin, the resurrection bringing a new being and a new heart.

Implicit in the doctrine of salvation was election. Edwards intended it to mean a sense of certification. Our salvation is certified—we know that it flows from the wellspring of God's mercy—when we know ourselves to have been elected to unite with Christ, "the head of all elected creatures" ("Remarks on Important Theological Controversies," II,538). Edwards' notion of election contained two things: foreknowledge and predestination. Choosing persons to be His own is what Edwards called God's "foreknowing of them"; destining them to be conformed to the image of Christ was God's predestination. "For God having in foreknowledge given us to Christ, he thenceforth beheld us as members and parts of him; and so ordaining the head [Christ] to glory, he therein ordained the members to glory" (II,538). In destining Christ to eternal life, he destined all parts of Christ as well. Edwards does not suggest that personal salvation is only a matter of one's uniting with the Spirit of God, or with whatever divine attributes—Beauty, Excellency, Goodness, Wholeness—one accords Him apart from Christ. Edwards' thinking is thoroughly Christological. No place is this fact more evident than when he declared that "Christ's election is the foundation of ours," just as his justification and glorification comprise our foundation too (II,528).

But doctrine alone fails to explain the mystery in God's inscrutable ways. Regarding this specific doctrine of election, Calvin himself had warned against a speculative approach, saying that if a person "audaciously" intrudes his logical analysis into it, "he will find nothing with which to satisfy his curiosity." "For it is not right," Calvin said, "that a man with impunity enquire into those things which the Lord has willed to remain hidden in Himself, and should seek to probe into that eternal ground of wisdom which God wills to be adored but not understood."[6] Edwards likewise knew the futility in using doctrine to reach religious knowledge. To say doctrinally that Christ's election is the foundation of our own had little meaning for Edwards unless at the heart of the matter we encounter Christ and know that through our election as chosen members of Christ our salvation is thereby grounded in God. Speculation could predicate this mystery, but only the sense of it in the redeemed heart could verify it. Edwards knew that at the core of religious experience, and as it were at the midpoint between justification and salvation, is grace—a mystery that defies doctrinal formulation and yet enables man to respond to God in belief. In this consent is his conversion, his new tendency of heart, enabling him to reach those spiritual insights that natural reason, because of its corruption, could never provide.

Grace, Edwards kept saying with undiminishing fervor, was God's special presence afforded only to His elect. It was the sublime working of the Spirit through Christ in the heart of the religious person. The fact of this special power or presence made all the difference between the natural and the regenerated man. Furthermore, it authenticated the Deity not only as the upholder and sustainer of the natural world but also as the redeemer of sinful man, as the God of regeneration who bestows true freedom and salvation. The grace by which man is transformed Edwards distinguished as special or saving grace. Unlike common grace—common to both saints and sinners, and manifested in good works—saving grace is a "peculiar kind or degree of operation or influence of God's spirit"; it is, he said, entirely different "in nature and kind" from anything found in non-Christians.[7]

Edwards brought together his ideas on the nature of saving grace in his *Treatise on Grace*, probably written during the Stockbridge years[8] but unknown until Alexander Grosart published it in Edinburgh over a hundred years later in 1865. At the time he discovered it, Grosart reported finding it "carefully finished and prepared for the press," and he rightfully called it a "treasure."[9] Few things that Edwards wrote surpass it in intellectual and rhetorical brilliance. Pulsating through it, moreover, is a certain religious enthusiasm that owes its presence to Edwards' own religious imagination and vision.

In this work he delineates natural man as a "stranger" to God's special grace, as one who knows no more about the things of the Spirit than a blind man knows about colors. In his own way natural man is "totally blind," because he is a stranger to Christ. Spiritual sight comes only in "communion with Christ," but, as Edwards stressed, "there is no communion without union." Changing his metaphor, Edwards spoke of a "holy seed," a divine principle, a small thing like a grain of mustard-seed, that comes into the heart, flourishes, and brings forth a new creature. Befitting a person who is raised from the dead, his life now "is not only in a greater degree, but it is all new."[10] The reader of the *Treatise* who pays careful attention to Edwards' figurative language will notice that the balance of phrase and rhythm keeps perfect pace with imagistic progression that moves from death to rebirth, separateness to communion, blindness to sight, the call to the response, nothingness to creation.

Climaxing the *Treatise* is Edwards' account of "the soul and essence and summary comprehension of all grace," the gift of all gifts, the principle of divine love "that is in the heart of the saints in the full extent, which primarily has God for its object."[11] As if captured and possessed by Paul's mounting cadences, Edwards writes:

> If a man does all these things here spoken, makes such glorious prophecies, has such knowledge, such faith, and speaks so excellently, and performs such excellent external acts, and does such great things in religion as giving all his goods to the poor and giving his body to be burned, what is wanting but one thing? The very quintessence of all religion, the very thing wherein lies summarily the sincerity, spirituality, and divinity of religion. And that, the Apostle teaches us, is LOVE.[12]

In defining such love Edwards acknowledged his linguistic limitations, confessing that things of this nature are not capable of definition, and that, in fact, "they are better felt than defined." Yet with repeated use of metaphor he tried with all his might. To have a sense of divine love in the heart is "the soul's relish of the supreme excellency of the divine nature, inclining the heart to God as the chief good"; this heartfelt sense causes one "to have a relish of the loveliness and sweetness" of God; the regenerate soul "is brought to see, or rather to taste, the superlative loveliness of the Divine Being"; finally, divine love is "holy oil . . . soft-flowing and diffusive . . . unparalleled [in] sweetness and fragrancy . . . like the precious ointment on the head, that ran down upon the beard, even Aaron's beard, that went down to the skirts of his garments."[13]

No brief summary can do justice to this remarkable piece, so rich in image and idea. Its successor, also published posthumously in 1865, was *The Nature of True Virtue*. Both works are sequels to the *Treatise Concerning Religious Affections*; in each, the subject is man before and after redemption. But whereas the *Treatise on Grace* shows its author filled with holy zeal, such that his prose becomes virtually that of religious language, *The Nature of True Virtue* is relentlessly logical and analytical, and only rarely is there figurative detail to suggest the exuberance behind its composition. At the conclusion of the *Treatise on Grace*, Edwards adumbrated the theme of this next work: " 'Tis the Spirit that is the only principle of true virtue in the heart. So that to be truly virtuous is the same as to be spiritual."[14] True virtue, therefore, consists in a oneness with God's Spirit, and its central principle is love. To be in union with God's love through Christ is to rest in the ultimate harmony of things. This is the gift of special grace lacking which no man can break out of the circle of self-love and unite with the infinitude of divine love.

Reading his tightly argued discussion of true virtue tempts one to conclude that Edwards' main concern is with ethics. Allen, for example, remarks that in this treatise Edwards "outlines the transition from theology to ethics."[15] In truth, Edwards leaves the reader to make his own transition, and Allen's judgment is valid only if we clearly see that Edwards intends experiential religion always to precede Christian ethics. In this treatise on true virtue he does not trace the practical applications of love or virtue, as he had done in the Twelfth Sign in *Religious Affections*. Instead he heralds love as an end in itself. His emphasis rests upon love of general being, not of particular beings. He distrusted so-called benevolent dispositions aimed at particular persons or corporate society. Such love, he said, "falls infinitely short of the universality of existence."[16] Love that only has for its object another person, a family, a society, or nation demonstrates at best a "selfish, contracted, narrow spirit"[17] and at worst a thoroughgoing enmity towards God. Such love in the last analysis is only self-love. It is merely ethical behavior lacking a religious basis. Again with Pauline overtones Edwards insisted that "no affection whatsoever to any creature, or any system of created beings, which is not dependent on, nor subordinate to a propensity or union of the heart to God, the supreme and infinite Being, can be of the nature of true virtue."[18] As in the *Treatise on Grace,* Edwards' unequivocal concern is divine love, God-centeredness, and the new sense of being that salvation promises. As opposed to natural affections which spring from human-centeredness and concern themselves only with what is particular and private, religious affections originate from the ontological power of divine love and fix themselves upon Being in general. To consent through grace to this dimension of reality is to unite with what Edwards called "the greatest share of existence," the excellency and love of God.[19]

Edwards' great themes consistently were those of grace, love, and salvation. A fundamental reason accounting for this has to do with Edwards' view of man. H. Richard Niebuhr has come closer than anyone else in pinpointing what this insight was. He asserts that "under the illumination of revelation" Edwards discerned something profoundly contradictory in the human spirit.[20] On the one hand he saw man as motivated by self-love—the morality of his fallen nature—but on the other hand as "one who feels he ought not to be as he is." Edwards saw that fallen man has a sense "that something is required of him which exceeds his present ability, namely, to be just and loyal in a truly universal sense with complete disinterestedness."[21] What Niebuhr suggests is that Edwards attributed to man a deep yearning for something that self-love failed to satisfy.

Just as Edwards' own vision of human history was the story of redemption from self-love to the love of all being, so, according to Niebuhr, he attributed to all men a yearning for a similar vision.

Niebuhr's provocative observation helps to explain not only Edwards' deep concern with sin but his even greater preoccupation with salvation. It was not dread of hell so much as the relish for heaven which Edwards thought to be man's universal temper. Even though fallen man's natural propensity inclines him away from God, there is still that sense of "ought" that enables him to respond through grace to the call of deliverance. Had Edwards lacked this confidence in the human response, he would have had to recognize the vanity in preaching on the theme of salvation. But having this assurance, he exhorted his listeners to act upon their sense of ought. In such sermons as "The Christian Pilgrim," "The Wisdom of God Displayed in the Way of Salvation," "Ruth's Resolution," and "Pressing Into the Kingdom" he held before his people the vision of Canaan. All the while he indefatigably helped them press towards it. Once the blessings are tasted, Edwards said, the more reason one has to press even further, until "we are brought to an immensely more exalted kind of union with God, and enjoyment of him, both the Father and the Son, than otherwise could have been" ("The Excellency of Christ," I,689). Ultimately the heavenly vision is union, without angels or saints as intercessors ("Heaven" from *Miscellaneous Observations*, II,630).

Edwards believed that deep in the consciousness of all men is an unquenchable ontological yearning, satisfied only by one's closing with Christ. In uniting with Christ, a man becomes a complete person, one who not only has passed beyond natural humanity but has experienced its redemption. Through faith he has been justified, and through the miraculous power of divine love—never, for Edwards, a mere feeling or emotion but rather an ontological force—he is blessed with new life, peace, and sight. This is the great theme of Edwards' sermon of August 1750, "The Peace Which Christ Gives His True Followers." He took his text from John 14:27—"Peace I leave with you, my peace I give unto you." He might also have chosen Paul's words in Romans 5:1—"Therefore being justified by faith, we have peace with God through our Lord Jesus Christ." Both passages designate the blessing of peace afforded the believer. Edwards supplied his own interpretive nuance to account for the nature of this peace. The peace Christians have, he said, "arises from their having their eyes open, and seeing things as they are" (II,91). He equated heart with sight, finding in the purity of one the essence of the other. The pure heart was the seeing heart. "God is the giver of the pure heart," Edwards wrote, "and he gives it for this very end; that it may be prepared for the blessedness of seeing him" ("The Pure in Heart Blessed," II,911). In the Christian sense, to be is to have sight, to apprehend God's presence and see His countenance.

3
Nature and History

It is not surprising that throughout Edwards' writing one finds natural images taken from the New England countryside. His was a "frontier childhood," as Ola Winslow points out, and at no time from his earliest years at East Windsor to his final ones at Stockbridge was he more than a short horseback ride from virgin forests and all manner of natural beauty.[22] When he came to write his *Personal Narrative*, he used prolific imagery of thunder, flowers, trees, sky, sun, and clouds. In the deservedly famous passage describing the soul (his own) of a true Christian, such imagery abounds:

> [The soul] appeared like such a little white flower as we see in the spring of the year; low and humble on the ground, opening its bosom to receive the pleasant beams of the sun's glory; rejoicing, as it were, in a calm rapture; diffusing around a sweet fragrancy; standing peacefully and lovingly, in the midst of other flowers round about; all in a like manner opening their bosoms to drink in the light of the sun. (I,lvi)

Characteristically he associated images of natural beauty with religious conversion. Another noteworthy example appears in his sermon "True Grace Distinguished from the Experience of Devils," in which he suggests a spirituality imbuing lambs and doves, jewels, lilies, plants of paradise, and stars of heaven, whereas he suggests the opposite in such images as the wolf, the lion, and the serpent (II,42-43).

There is nothing particularly significant in this. Sensory language is commonly used to describe states of being, whether psychological or spiritual. What is more important is the way Edwards beheld nature itself. Something more than metaphor is at work when he describes John the Baptist as the first day-star and Christ as the effulgent sun that ascends ever higher until "the day-star itself gradually disappears" ("Pressing Into the Kingdom," I,654); or when in another sermon he speaks of the saints as lights shining "with the glory of Christ reflected from them" ("The Portion of the Righteous," II,898). More than an image restricted to metaphor, "sunlight" is rather a "type," an image of a divine thing. Implanted into the natural phenomenon of light is Edwards' prior vision of Christ. That Puritans were less imagists than allegorists is demonstrated in the way they brought *a priori* religious truths to nature rather than using nature as the means to such truths.[23] Edwards' practice had to do first with religious experience and only then with a vision of nature as such. Before he could see "sunlight" as the image or emanation of a divine thing, he first had to have experienced Christ as a divine truth. Thus in the distinction between metaphor and emanation, sunlight as metaphor is analogous to that which the human mind conceives, whereas sunlight as emanation issues forth from the divine mind and is perceived through the clarity of purified vision. Beheld in this new way, sunlight and all nature exist within the unity of divine meaning. Everything proceeds from God, as light from the sun.

The divine pattern Edwards perceived in nature had its counterpart in history. Seen through the same regenerate imagination and vision, history delivered a unified meaning. Like nature it was a "type" or emanation revealing God's purpose in creation. To decipher history typologically meant to see each event not only in a continuum of human activity but also in cosmic significance. Even though both nature and history constituted only the world of everyday life and therefore lacked ultimate reality, they were still meaningful types of God's excellency.

Edwards' view of history, like his view of nature, rested upon the conviction that the heart determines perception. Religious experience shapes what we perceive in history, and thus the account of history is to be written from the standpoint of what is pertinent to the truth and destiny of the believer's life. Edwards held that the events in history, when interpreted by the believing spirit, are not capricious but intelligible according to an integrating purpose and direction. Events coalesce into a unified whole showing what God has done; their historicity is based upon the actions of God's people. The overall pattern reveals God's "great design." Religious imagination interacts with revelation to show all events as part and parcel of salvation history.

In a series of sermons delivered in 1739 and published posthumously in 1774 as *A History of the Work of Redemption,* Edwards set forth what he envisioned as the "great design." History, he wrote, consists of "many successive works and dispensations of God, all tending to one great effect, united as the several parts of a scheme, and all together making up one great work" (I,535). Its singular meaning is God's work of redemption ("The work of redemption and the work of salvation are the same thing"— I,534). In this majestic purpose nothing is fortuitous, nothing is apart from God's will, nothing is accidental. Divine foreknowledge and predestination, doctrines which Edwards associated with the doctrine of election, were thus bound up with his view of history.

Joseph Haroutunian, writing about Calvin's doctrine of predestination, warns against interpreting it as merely deterministic. The same warning applies to Edwards' concept of history. Determinism, Haroutunian reminds us, means simply that one fact arises from another "by way of a natural necessity" which we can discover and understand. But, he says, we cannot arrive at an understanding of predestination by studying the condition of Christians in this world. No comprehensible explanation accounts for God's ways. "God's purpose remains God's secret, and he alone can justify his deeds among men."[24] Edwards' concept presupposes the same mystery infusing all history. No theory of determinism, no study of cause and effect, can account for it. The mystery is that of salvation, affirmed by the heart and its oneness with Christ.

That Edwards divided history into epochs after the manner of Augustine in the *City of God* did not lessen the essential mystery from which he believed history emanates. For Peter Gay to state that even though Edwards' mind was neither reactionary nor fundamentalist "yet his history was"[25] suggests a cleavage between perception and percept, between the envisioning mind and what the mind envisions. Were Edwards' epochs mere objective (fundamentalist) history, such a cleavage would have been implicit. Or were they the result of "enlightened history," such as was being written by Hume, Voltaire, and Gibbon, then a person might justifiably question the unitary consistency of Edwards' perception and discovery. For Edwards the epochs constituting the overall design signified something akin to mythical consciousness, just as Biblical history is mythical in its narration of what God and His people have done and in its account of God's revelation to them.[26] Yet Edwards' interpretation of history represented a still further visionary design dependent upon the mystery of revelation and grace. In it he accounted for human events in terms of creation and eschatology, the covenant of grace, and the total work of salvation. Accordingly, in Edwards' view the *first* period, from "the fall of man to the incarnation of Christ," was a time when God was preparing for Christ's coming; the *second* period, from "Christ's incarnation to his resurrection," was when the Savior procured and purchased redemption; and the *third* period, extending from "the resurrection of Christ to the end of the world," is to be taken up in accomplishing the final redemptive purpose (I,535). These epochs represented something more than Edwards' indebtedness to Biblical sources and Augustine. They were coherent stages in God's moral government seen from the perspective of Edwards' regenerate eye.

Edwards divided the so-called third period into seven parts, the first six delineating the suffering church in history, and the seventh its final victory. They were: (1) from Christ's resurrection to the destruction of Jerusalem; (2) from the destruction of Jerusalem to Constantine; (3) from Constantine to the rise of the Antichrist (the papacy); (4) from the rise of the Antichrist to the Reformation; (5) from the Reformation to the present time; (6) from the present time to the fall of the Antichrist (Revelation 61:1ff.); (7) the millennium, a period of a thousand years, a golden age for the church on earth—from the fall of the Antichrist to the second coming of Christ, the resurrection of the dead, judgment, and the consummation when the wicked will suffer eternally and the elect will join together in their New Jerusalem.

Edwards' contributions to eschatology occur in his speculations concerning the millennium.[27] Like the Reformers, who believed that the enemies of Christ (the Turks and the papacy) would be crushed before the last day,[28] Edwards believed that within history and before Christ's return Satan's "visible kingdom" will be destroyed: "the very wind will carry it away as the chaff of the summer threshing-floor" (I,607). All heresies will be abolished. Socinianism, Arianism, Quakerism, Arminianism, Deism ("which is now so bold and confident in infidelity") shall be crushed; "Satan's Mahometan kingdom" and "Jewish infidelity" shall be overthrown (I,607-608). All regions of the earth—Africa, the East Indies, etc.—will be inhabited by holy people, and the vast continent of America will be covered "with glorious gospel-light and Christian love" (I,608). Like Calvin, confident that the Gospel "would make progress throughout the whole world" and Christ the King would achieve victory over Satan and sin,[29] and like the English Puritans who found this view of history "most acceptable and developed it,"[30] Edwards also expressed millennial hopes having soteriological consequences.

Of particular interest are Edwards' hopes about America. Alan Heimert in his study of religion in America pays careful attention to Edwards' eschatology concerning God's work not only in individual lives but in society. For Edwards the key event in America, of course, was the Great Awakening. According to Heimert, it was the Awakening that Edwards had in mind when in *The Nature of True Virtue* he described the sight "of a society or system of intelligent beings, sweetly united in benevolent agreement of heart."[31] Heimert also suggests that *Religious Affections*, commonly regarded as having to do with individual religious experience, encompasses a broader area including God's work of redemption in the world as well as in America during the 1740's.[32]

In his 1739 sermons Edwards cited America as the land where someday Christian love would reign. He saw the tantalizing dawn of such a time. Three years after delivering his sermons on redemption, he reaffirmed the probability that millennial glory "will begin in America" (*Thoughts*, 353). He interpreted the "isles" referred to in Isaiah 60:9—"Surely the isles shall wait for me"—as America. The work now begun, he said, "if it should go on and prevail . . . would make New England a kind of heaven upon the earth" (*Thoughts*, 385). The vision had lost none of its clarity when in 1747 he wrote *An Humble Attempt to Promote Explicit Agreement and Visible Union of God's People, in Extraordinary Prayer, for the Revival of Religion and the Advancement of Christ's Kingdom on Earth*. In this work he applauded the two-year effort of Scottish ministers in Edinburgh, Glasgow, Aberdeen, and Dundee to have congregations join in a Concert of Prayer at certain common times, and he recommended the practice to American congregations. Edwards was confident that the fall of the Antichrist was not far off, and glorious days were soon to come to America. Perry Miller observes that the *Humble Attempt* provides clues to Edwards' "fascination" with the doctrine of the millennium and the triumph to be achieved "on earth."[33] Two years later, when Edwards published his *Humble Inquiry into the Qualifications for Communion* (1749), the millennial hopes were still bright, this time concerning an ecclesiastical polity in New England that supposedly would not only settle the controversy about communion but would hasten the coming of the Kingdom. Heimert notes that the *Humble Inquiry* was "clearly cast in an eschatological framework" which presupposed the church as a "type," an "image," a "faint resemblance" of the millennium and, like the Concert of Prayer proposed in the earlier document, " 'a forerunner of that future joy' and an instrument for bringing it into being."[34]

In keeping pace with his millennial outlook, we need not be detained by Edwards' own dream for America. In the next century that dream had ample spokesmen, who in secularizing it became, as Goen says, "activists in its fulfillment from sea to shining sea."[35] The great nineteenth-century vision conceived of America as the kingdom of God, its towns and villages—New Hope, Concord, Zion, New Harmony, etc.—bearing names testifying to this fulfillment. Miller is right of course in suggesting that that dream ended once and for all at 0815 hours on 6 August, 1945, in the boil of flame that engulfed Hiroshima[36] —a conflagration, he implies, that is not irrelevant to Edwards' apocalyptic vision of the destruction following the golden age and then the judgment when, once the saints have ascended into eternal glory, "this world shall be set on fire, and be turned into a furnace" (*History of Redemption*, I,614).

Edwards' higher vision, whether as millennial or apocalyptic, swept beyond America's destiny to encompass God's purpose in creation. It was a majestic panorama that Edwards never lived to finish writing. Published posthumously in 1765 as *A Dissertation Concerning the End for Which God Created the World*, the piece was only a fragment of what he had intended to be his *chef-d'ouevre*. Yet like the other unfinished work (*The Nature of True Virtue*) which was published with it, there is sufficient content to show Edwards "at his very greatest."[37] His editor, probably Samuel Hopkins, noted in his Preface that the subjects handled in both fragments "are sublime and important," also noting that the reader may find it difficult to keep pace with the writer "where the ascent is arduous" (I,94).

Edwards defined true virtue as a propensity of the heart for God. True virtue consists in genuine benevolence to Being (or love of God). With a certain audacity Edwards also defined God's own virtue as consisting primarily in love of Himself—"in the mutual love and friendship which subsists eternally and necessarily between the several persons in the Godhead."[38] God's final purpose, therefore, is not in effecting man's happiness, as the Arminians held, but in revealing His own glory. Regarding God's nature, Edwards established an original disposition "to an emanation of his own infinite fulness . . . so that the emanation itself was arrived at by him as a last end of the creation" (*Concerning the End,* I,100). What God seeks and accomplishes, beyond the redemption of the world, is the display of His own being. His excellency is the final cause and motive of the world. The stupendous drama of man's fall and subsequent redemption through Christ reaches its loftiest point when the elect see God's infinite fullness in all things and unite in its divine perfection. To participate in God's knowledge, love, and joy of Himself is the essence of Christian knowledge, love, and joy.

God's ultimate purpose is to reveal Himself, and the essence of Christian experience is to participate in the revelation. Edwards achieved consummate vision when, with characteristic imagery of light, he described this revelation:

> As there is an infinite fulness of all possible good in God—a fulness of every perfection, of all excellency and beauty, and of infinite happiness—and as this fulness is capable of communication, or emanation *ad extra;* so it seems a thing amiable and valuable in itself that this infinite fountain of good should send forth abundant streams. . . . Thus it is fit, since there is an infinite fountain of light and knowledge, that this light should shine forth in beams of communicated knowledge and understanding; and, as there is an infinite fountain of holiness, moral excellence, and beauty, that so it should flow out in communicated holiness. And that, as there is an

infinite fulness of joy and happiness, so these should have an emanation, and become a fountain flowing out in abundant streams, as beams from the sun. (*Concerning the End*, I,99-100)

The passage illustrates what Elwood perceptively identifies as Edwards' "higher synthesis," which does justice both to the majesty and separateness of God (Puritan Calvinism) and to the immediacy of His presence (Cambridge Platonism). Elwood sees in this synthesis the anticipation of Whitehead's process philosophy and the existential reinterpretation of Reformation theology, both hallmarks of contemporary theological concern.[39]

4

The Glory of God

What the fullness of Edwards' own *summa theologica* would have been like, had he lived to finish writing it, we can only guess. Yet even as a fragment, *Concerning the End* was "concisely sketched out" (Hopkins' Preface, I,94) so as to conclude on the theme of God's glory. The higher synthesis Edwards achieved came with the conception of this work. Edwards' noblest concept is the glory of God. It demanded a passionate devotion and a profoundly integrated mind, qualities Haroutunian finds admirably distinct in Edwards, whom God indeed had blessed "with a unique sense and knowledge of his Glory."[40]

Edwards identified God's ultimate end in creating the world as the emanation and communication of His infinite fullness. The ultimate end of creation is God Himself. In this consummatory vision Edwards also recognized manifold distinctions that needed clarification. In considering emanation, for example, he explained that we must also think about the "exercise" of God's perfection and the "effect" of it, the subtle distinctions between divine manifestation and divine communication, and our own "esteem" of God's ways, including our "exercise and expressions" of this esteem (I,119). Struggling with the problem of how to express the ineffable, Edwards conjoined all these various aspects into the one term "glory." In this term his theology reached finality—but a finality which even yet remained obscure because of the unavoidable "imperfection of language to express things of so sublime a nature" (I,119).

Two aspects of the term, however, Edwards stressed with both confidence and faith. One was the divine attribute of light. All beauty, love, and joy in all their divine fullness come together in a single effulgence or shining brightness: "The glory of the Lord shone round about them" (Luke 2:9). Inseparable in this vision of light is the experiential knowledge of God's excellency. The emanation or effulgence of brightness belongs to the eye of the beholder; light "has relation to the sense of seeing" (I,118). Therefore, the glory of God includes both His transcendent majesty and His presence in the human heart, both His emanation and man's salvation. The overflowing fullness of God's glory unites with the sense of it in the redeemed heart. Emanation and participation are indivisible. Being is available only through participation in true Being, just as light is real only in its being seen. First in divine emanation and then in human consent does the glory of God confirm the truth that God does all and man does all. Thus we are prepared for Edwards' crowning insight concerning the glory of God: "It is the abundant, extensive emanation and communication of the fulness of the sun to innumberable beings that partake of it. . . . It is by this that all nature receives life, comfort, and joy" (I,119).

Conclusion

Edwards lived during a time when increasing numbers of his American contemporaries saw no discrepancy between divine justice and human reason, between God's glory and man's goodness. It was a time when the American mainstream had divided, the one branch seeming to flow and spread out everywhere, nourishing the land with fructifying promises; the other branch—darker, deeper, more mysterious and threatening—went underground even while the unsuspecting people believed it to have vanished for good. The country would soon herald its political independence, and a few decades later its cultural independence. Emerson would then announce that America would no longer sing the courtly muses of the past but would write its own songs in its own idiom, as Whitman was to do in "Song of Myself." The political rights of man would become his new divinity; his mind as well as his country's marvelous landscape would serve as his *sanctum sanctorum*. In short, it was the best of times when prospects of the future seemed to make irrelevant the remembrances of things past.

Edwards, however, sought to keep those remembrances alive. He dared to have his congregation look to their Puritan past and to accept its burden, including its orthodox theology. He insisted that what Calvin had said about human sin and God's sovereign justice could not be eclipsed by the deceptive promises of free will and nationhood. For what Calvin had envisioned was a far more important drama than any unfolding in Philadelphia's Independence Hall or in the Boston countinghouses. That Edwards' mind was dominated by this other drama led him to preach that these were indeed the worst of times. Man's inheritance was burdened with sin, and only through God's redeeming grace could he be freed from endless curse.

Many students have tried to understand Edwards through the Northampton tragedy that sent him into the wilderness when his parishioners could no longer accept the painful reminders with which he confronted them. This interpretation is usually meant to show Edwards upholding a spent theology in an eighteenth-century nation that was rushing heaven-bent towards liberal democracy and universal benevolence. What the interpretation excludes is an epistemological vision extending to far greater reaches. Traditional though this vision was, it was also different and radical, informed by insights that reached back to man's beginnings and ahead to his end, back to creation and ahead to God's all-fulfilling glory. It was a religious vision encompassing these ultimate dimensions of reality. Thus Edwards believed that only the religious person is complete, for only such a person has envisioned the antipodes.

Edwards' theology records his own spiritual journeyings from darkness to light. Although his writings demonstrate intellectual discipline, finely honed logic, and reasoned argument of the highest order, their central theme concerns religious knowledge as held not in the head but in the heart. Edwards believed that only through the sense of the heart was man able to know the depths and the heights, and only in this way was he able to go beyond the tragedy implicit in human limitation. That Edwards seldom made his writings overtly autobiographical does not hide the great wellspring of heart and mind that impelled his work. As if corroborating the Calvinist irony, Edwards plunged into those dark waters and discovered his sunlit apotheosis. What this means theologically is that by virtue of the believer's union with Christ he has come to possess all things.

Notes

Chapter 1

1. *The Works of Jonathan Edwards*, with a Memoir by Sereno E. Dwight, ed. Edward Hickman, 2 vols. (London: F. Westley and A. H. Davis, 1834), I, lxxviii. Hereafter, reference to these volumes will be included in the text and placed within parentheses.

2. John Macquarrie, *An Existentialist Theology: A Comparison of Heidegger and Bultmann* (London: SCM Press, 1955), pp. 18-20.

3. Leon Howard, *"The Mind" of Jonathan Edwards: A Reconstructed Text* (Berkeley and Los Angeles: University of California Press, 1963), pp. 6-7.

4. *Ibid.*, p. 4.

5. Samuel Hopkins, *The Life of President Edwards*, in *The Works of President Edwards*, 8 vols. (Leeds, England: Edward Baines, 1806-1811), I, 11.

6. Ola Elizabeth Winslow, *Jonathan Edwards, 1703-1758* (New York: The Macmillan Company, 1940), pp. 63-64.

7. Edwards, in Howard, pp. 36, 64, 73.

8. *Ibid.*, p. 45.

9. *Ibid.*, p. 82.

10. *Ibid.*, pp. 83, 84.

11. *Ibid.*, p. 84 (my italics).

12. *The Philosophy of Jonathan Edwards from His Private Notebooks*, ed. Harvey G. Townsend (Eugene: University of Oregon Press, 1955). For an important discussion of Item #782 from the "Miscellanies" ("IDEAS, SENSE OF THE HEART, SPIRITUAL KNOWLEDGE OR CONVICTION, FAITH"), see Perry Miller, "Jonathan Edwards on the Sense of the Heart," *Harvard Theological Review*, XLI (April 1948), 123-145.

13. Howard, p. x; Edwards, in Howard, pp. 50, 52.

14. Perry Miller, *Jonathan Edwards* (Cleveland: World Publishing Company, 1959), p. 52.

15. Miller, "Jonathan Edwards on the Sense of the Heart," *Harvard Theological Review*, XLI (April 1948), 124.

16. *Ibid.*

17. Miller, *Jonathan Edwards*, p. 55.

18. John Locke, *An Essay Concerning Human Understanding*, 2 vols. (London: G. Offar, *et al.*, 1819), Book II, ch. i, section 2.

19. *Ibid.*, II,i,4.

20. *Ibid.*, II,xii,1.

21. "In efficacious grace we are not merely passive, nor yet does God do some, and we do the rest. But God does all and we do all. God produces all, and we act all. God is the only proper author and fountain; we are the proper

actors. We are, in different respects, wholly passive, and wholly active"—
Concerning Efficacious Grace, in *The Works of President Edwards*, 4 vols.
(New York: Robert Carter and Brothers, 1869), II, 581.
22. Joseph Haroutunian, review of Perry Miller, *Jonathan Edwards*, in *Theology Today*, VII (January 1951), 555.
23. William James, *The Varieties of Religious Experience: A Study in Human Nature* (London: Longmans, Green, and Co., 1902), p. 2.
24. *Ibid.*, p. 4.
25. *Ibid.*, pp. 6, 22.
26. *Ibid.*, p. 9.
27. *Ibid.*
28. John E. Smith, ed., Jonathan Edwards, *A Treatise Concerning Religious Affections* (New Haven: Yale University Press, 1959), p. 46.
29. "The Future Punishment of the Wicked Unavoidable and Intolerable," in *Works*, ed. Hickman, II, 78.
30. James, p. 9.

Chapter 2

1. Perry Miller, "Jonathan Edwards on the Sense of the Heart," *Harvard Theological Review*, XLI (April 1948), 124.
2. C. A. Patrides, ed., *The Cambridge Platonists* (London: Edward Arnold, Ltd., 1969), p. 28.
3. Joseph Haroutunian, "Jonathan Edwards: A Study in Godliness," *Journal of Religion*, XI (July 1931), 400, 403.
4. Miller, "Jonathan Edwards on the Sense of the Heart," 124.
5. *Ibid.*
6. Herbert Wallace Schneider, *The Puritan Mind* (London: Constable and Company, 1931, ch. 3.
7. *Ibid.*, p. 97.
8. *Ibid.*, p. 102.
9. Perry Miller, *Jonathan Edwards* (Cleveland: World Publishing Company, 1959), p. 29; Ola Elizabeth Winslow, *Jonathan Edwards, 1703-1758* (New York: The Macmillan Company, 1940), p. 152; Alexander V. G. Allen, *Jonathan Edwards* (Boston: Houghton, Mifflin and Company, 1889), p. 57.
10. Miller, *Jonathan Edwards*, p. 44. Frank Hugh Foster, in *A Genetic History of New England Theology* (New York: Russell & Russell, 1963), p. 52, combines this sermon with "God Glorified in Man's Dependence" to say that these two sermons were like "the first booming of a solitary gun upon the opening of a great battle."
11. John Calvin, *Commentaries*, ed. Joseph Haroutunian, in The Library of Christian Classics (London: SCM Press, Ltd., 1958), pp. 132-133.
12. Heinrich Emil Brunner, *Revelation and Reason*, trans. O. Wyon (London: Westminster, 1946), p. 79. The classic Brunner-Barth debate on this subject is found in Brunner and Karl Barth, *Natural Theology*, trans. Peter Fraenkel, with intro. by John Baillie (London: G. Bles, 1956). Brunner's essay is entitled, "Nature and Grace"; Barth's is "No!"
13. Jonathan Edwards, *Treatise on Grace*, from *Selections from the Unpub-*

lished Writings of Jonathan Edwards of America, ed. Alexander B. Grosart (Edinburgh, 1865), p. 25.

14. Calvin, *Commentaries,* p. 232. For Calvin's fuller treatment of justification through faith in Christ, see *Institutes of the Christian Religion,* 2 vols., ed. John T. McNeill, in The Library of Christian Classics (London: SCM Press, Ltd., 1960), III, xiv, 1-21. A helpful discussion of Calvin's interpretation of this doctrine is found in Wilhelm Niesel, *The Theology of Calvin,* trans. Harold Knight (London: Lutterworth Press, 1956), pp. 130-137.

15. The classic definition of the Covenant Theology in America is Perry Miller's "The Marrow of Puritan Divinity," *Publications of the Colonial Society of Massachusetts,* XXXII (1937), 247-300, reprinted in Miller, *Errand Into the Wilderness* (New York: Harper & Row, 1964), pp. 48-98.

16. Miller, *Jonathan Edwards,* p. 79.

17. *Ibid.*

18. Foster, p. 3.

19. Jonathan Edwards, *The Great Awakening,* ed. C. C. Goen (New Haven: Yale University Press, 1972). The title is that established by Goen. The volume contains Edwards' *A Faithful Narrative* (1737), *The Distinguishing Marks* (1741), *Some Thoughts Concerning the Revival* (1743), letters, and prefaces. Subsequent references to the three main works of Edwards included in this volume will be to the Goen edition and will appear within parentheses in the text.

20. Goen, ed., p. 90.

21. Winslow, p. 167.

22. F. O. Matthiessen, *American Renaissance* (New York: Oxford University Press, 1941), p. 279.

23. C. S. Lewis, *Christian Reflections,* ed. Walter Hooper (Grand Rapids, Michigan: William B. Eerdmans Publishing Company, 1967), p. 116.

24. Alan Heimert, *Religion and the American Mind: From the Great Awakening to the Revolution* (Cambridge, Mass.: Harvard University Press, 1966), p. 40.

25. Calvin, *Commentaries,* p. 126.

26. Calvin, *Institutes of the Christian Religion,* III, ii, 36; I, vii, 5.

27. Miller, *Jonathan Edwards,* p. 177.

28. Jonathan Edwards, *A Treatise Concerning Religious Affections,* ed. John R. Smith (New Haven: Yale University Press, 1959). Subsequent references to this edition will appear within parentheses in the text.

29. See Sam Keen, *To a Dancing God* (New York: Harper & Row, 1970); Harvey Cox, *Feast of Fools: A Theological Essay on Festivity & Fantasy* (Cambridge, Mass.: Harvard University Press, 1969).

30. Calvin, *Commentaries,* p. 133.

31. William James, *The Varieties of Religious Experience: A Study in Human Nature* (London: Longmans, Green, and Co., 1902), p. 20.

32. *Ibid.,* pp. 238, 239.

33. Søren Kierkegaard, *The Sickness Unto Death,* in *Fear and Trembling/The Sickness . . .* (New York: Doubleday & Co., 1954), p. 145.

34. James Carse, *Jonathan Edwards and the Visibility of God* (New York: Charles Scribner's Sons, 1967), p. 149.

35. Miller, *Jonathan Edwards,* pp. 209-223.

36. Calvin, *Institutes,* IV,xv,14.

Chapter 3

1. Jonathan Edwards, "Miscellanies," in *The Philosophy of Jonathan Edwards from His Private Notebooks*, ed. Harvey G. Townsend (Eugene: University of Oregon, 1955), p. 115.
2. "The distribution [Edwards wrote] of the human knowledge into speculative and sensible . . . indeed may be extended to all the knowledge we have of all objects whatsoever. For there is no kind of thing that we know but what may be considered as in some respect or other concerning the wills or hearts of spiritual beings. And indeed we are concerned to know nothing on any other account. So that perhaps this distinction of the kinds of our knowledge into speculative and sensible, if duly weighed, will be found the most important of all" (*ibid.*, p. 120).
3. Edwards, in Perry Miller, "Jonathan Edwards on the Sense of the Heart," *Harvard Theological Review*, XLI (April 1948), 142. The major substance of this article (pp. 129-145) consists of an excerpt (Item 782) from Edwards' "Miscellanies"; Edwards entitled this Item, "IDEAS, SENSE OF THE HEART, SPIRITUAL KNOWLEDGE OR CONVICTION. FAITH."
4. *Ibid.*, 143.
5. Douglas J. Elwood, *The Philosophical Theology of Jonathan Edwards* (New York: Columbia University Press, 1960), p. 136.
6. "The Divine and Supernatural Light," II,14; *Religious Affections*, p. 272. When referring to either (1) *The Works of Jonathan Edwards*, ed. Edward Hickman (London: F. Westley and A. H. Davis, 1834), 2 vols., or (2) *A Treatise Concerning Religious Affections*, ed. John E. Smith (New Haven: Yale University Press, 1959), I will continue to follow the practice used in the earlier chapters by inserting documentation within the written text.
7. Edwards, in Miller, "Jonathan Edwards on the Sense of the Heart," 144.
8. See William F. Lynch, *Christ and Apollo: The Dimensions of the Literary Imagination* (New York: New American Library, 1963), p. 28.
9. Edwards' "Of the Prejudices of the Imagination" is included in Leon Howard, *"The Mind" of Jonathan Edwards: A Reconstructed Text* (Berkeley and Los Angeles: University of California Press, 1963), pp. 146-148. Edwards' reference to the rationalists appears on p. 147; Howard's terms appear on p. 133.
10. Perry Miller, *Jonathan Edwards* (Cleveland: World Publishing Company, 1959), p. 180. R. W. B. Lewis also sees Edwards as a "mediator" in his effort to use Locke and Newton to restore Calvinism. It was this double-edged enterprise that "lent drama to Edwards' role"; it was "his attempt to mediate that gave rise to the drama"—*The American Adam: Innocence, Tragedy and Tradition in the Nineteenth Century* (Chicago: University of Chicago Press, 1958), p. 63.
11. Edwards, "Mysteries of Scriptures," in *The Works of President Edwards*, 4 vols. (New York: Robert Carter and Brothers, 1869), III, 540.
12. Northrop Frye, *The Educated Imagination* (Bloomington: Indiana University Press, 1964), pp. 105, 80.
13. Friedrich Nietzsche, *The Birth of Tragedy/The Genealogy of Morals*, in one volume, trans. Francis Golffing (Garden City, N. Y.: Doubleday & Co., 1956), pp. 52, 60, 107, 140, 180.

14. Roland André Delattre, *Beauty and Sensibility in the Thought of Jonathan Edwards: An Essay in Aesthetics and Theological Ethics* (New Haven: Yale University Press, 1968), pp. 29, 119-121, 146.

15. H. Richard Niebuhr, *The Meaning of Revelation* (New York: The Macmillan Company, 1941), p. 101.

16. Edwards, "Observations Concerning Faith," in *The Works of President Edwards*, II, 606.

17. See Immanuel Kant, Preface to Second Edition, *Critique of Pure Reason*, trans. Norman Kemp Smith (London: Macmillan and Co., 1929), pp. 17-37. In his *Commentary to Kant's 'Critique of Pure Reason'* (London: Macmillan and Co., 1923), Smith observes that Kant did not make empirical knowledge "coextensive with human insight" (p. lv).

18. Edwards, in *The Philosophy of Jonathan Edwards from His Private Notebooks*, ed. Townsend, p. 111.

19. Richard Kroner, *The Religious Function of Imagination* (New Haven: Yale University Press, 1941), p. 37.

20. *Ibid.*, p. 39.

21. Jonathan Edwards, *Images and Shadows of Divine Things*, ed. Perry Miller (New Haven: Yale University Press, 1948). See Miller's introduction, pp. 1-41.

22. *Ibid.*, pp. 45, 46, 101, 128.

23. Spirit that transcends matter "is reached by a special faculty, the *intuitus* of the Scholastics"—Herbert Read, *Icon and Idea: The Function of Art in the Development of Human Consciousness* (London: Faber and Faber, Ltd., 1955), p. 64.

24. Samuel Taylor Coleridge, *Biographia Literaria*, 2 vols. (London: Rest Fenner, 1817), I, 202.

25. Miller, in Edwards, *Images and Shadows of Divine Things*, p. 2.

26. Jacques Maritain, *Creative Intuition in Art and Poetry* (Cleveland: World Publishing Company, 1954), pp. 177-178.

27. *Ibid.*, pp. 180-181.

28. Ralph Waldo Emerson, "Nature" (Section IV), in *Selections from Ralph Waldo Emerson*, ed. Stephen E. Whicher (Boston: Houghton Mifflin Company, 1957), p. 31.

29. C. S. Lewis, *Christian Reflections*, ed. Walter Hooper (Grand Rapids, Michigan: William B. Eerdmans Publishing Company, 1967), p. 8.

30. The bibliography on this subject is growing rapidly. The best recent survey of relevant studies is found in Amos Wilder's introduction to his *Early Christian Rhetoric: The Language of the Gospel* (Cambridge, Mass.: Harvard University Press, 1971). His earlier volume, *Theology and Modern Literature* (Cambridge, Mass.: Harvard University Press, 1958), is instructive. The most prolific scholar in this field is Nathan A. Scott, Jr.; his many books on the subject include *The Broken Center: Studies in the Theological Horizon of Modern Literature* (New Haven: Yale University Press, 1968); *Negative Capability: Studies in the New Literature and the Religious Situation* (New Haven: Yale University Press, 1969); *The Wild Prayer of Longing: Poetry and the Sacred* (New Haven: Yale University Press, 1971). Another recent study is T. R. Henn, *The Bible as Literature* (London: Oxford University Press, 1970).

31. Austin Farrer argues that analysis of the Gospel of St. Mark "belongs plainly to the criticism of poetry," which is its genre—*The Glass of Vision*

(London: Dacre Press, 1948), p. 145. Although Helen Gardner attacks Farrer on several points, she also thinks that "reading the Gospel is like reading a poem"—*The Business of Criticism* (London: Oxford University Press, 1959), p. 102. For an analysis of the Bible as archetype, see Northrop Frye, *The Anatomy of Criticism* (Princeton: Princeton University Press, 1957), pp. 315-326.

32. John W. Dixon, "The Matter of Theology: The Consequences of Art for Theological Method," *The Journal of Religion,* XLIX (April 1969), 173.

33. Paul Tillich, *Theology of Culture,* ed. Robert C. Kimball (New York: Oxford University Press, 1959), p. 68. See Gabriel Vahanian, "Picasso's Iconoclasm," *The Christian Century,* LXXXVIII (December 29, 1971), 1523-1525, for a further discussion of this subject.

34. T. S. Eliot, *The Sacred Wood: Essays on Poetry and Criticism* (London: Methuen & Co., Ltd., 1920), pp. 144-155.

35. Perry Miller, *The New England Mind: The Seventeenth Century* (Cambridge, Mass.: Harvard University Press, 1954), p. 6.

36. *Ibid.,* ch. 1, "The Augustinian Strain of Piety."

37. Miller, *Jonathan Edwards,* p. 328.

38. Samuel Perkins Hayes, "An Historical Study of the Edwardean Revivals," *The American Journal of Psychology,* XIII (October 1902), 558; Joseph Haroutunian, "Jonathan Edwards: Theologian of the Great Commandment," *Theology Today,* I (April 1944), 367; Edwin H. Cady, "The Artistry of Jonathan Edwards," *New England Quarterly,* XXII (March 1949), 61-72; Delattre, *Beauty and Sensibility in the Thought of Jonathan Edwards.*

39. E. M. W. Tillyard and C. S. Lewis, *The Personal Heresy: A Controversy* (London: Oxford University Press, 1965), p. 89.

40. Haroutunian, "Jonathan Edwards: Theologian of the Great Commandment," p. 368.

41. Gerardus van der Leeuw, *Sacred and Profane Beauty: The Holy in Art,* trans. David E. Green (New York: Holt, Rinehart and Winston, 1963), p. 284.

42. W. H. Auden, *The Dyer's Hand and Other Essays* (New York: Random House, 1962), p. 457.

43. *Ibid.*

44. Lewis, *Christian Reflections,* p. 67.

45. George Santayana, *Interpretations of Poetry and Religion* (New York: Harper & Brothers, 1957), p. 92.

46. *Ibid.,* p. 94.

47. Santayana, p. 89; G. Wilson Knight, *The Christian Renaissance* (New York: W. W. Norton & Co., 1962), p. 33; Kroner, p. 47.

48. Calvin, *Commentaries,* ed. Joseph Haroutunian, in Library of Christian Classics (London: SCM Press, Ltd., 1958), pp. 175-176. Both Edwards and Calvin affirm that only through faith is the invisible divinity made manifest, and that "we have not the eyes to see this unless they be illumined by the inner revelation of God through faith"—see Calvin, *Institutes,* I,v,14. For a monumental study of religious vision, consult Rudolf Otto, *The Idea of the Holy,* 2nd ed., trans. John W. Harvey (London: Oxford University Press, 1950).

49. Miller, *Jonathan Edwards,* ch. 3, "The Objective Good."

Chapter 4

1. Jonathan Edwards, in Leon Howard, *"The Mind" of Jonathan Edwards: A Reconstructed Text* (Berkeley and Los Angeles: University of California Press, 1963), p. 139.
2. Edwards in Howard, *ibid.*, p. 141.
3. Jonathan Edwards, in *The Philosophy of Jonathan Edwards from His Private Notebooks*, ed. Harvey G. Townsend (Eugene: University of Oregon Press, 1955), p. 115.
4. *Ibid.*, p. 210.
5. *Ibid.*
6. Analogical language as related to "types" and, philosophically, to Edwards' notion of consent of being to Being (in *The Nature of True Virtue*) may be profitably studied in Paul R. Baumgartner, "Jonathan Edwards: The Theory Behind His Use of Figurative Language," *PMLA*, LXXVIII (September 1963), 321-325.
7. Edwards, in *The Philosophy. . .* , ed. Townsend, p. 210.
8. Perry Miller, *Jonathan Edwards* (Cleveland: World Publishing Company, 1959), pp. 157-158.
9. Jonathan Edwards, *Observations Concerning Faith*, in *The Works of President Edwards*, 4 vols. (New York: Robert Carter and Brothers, 1869), II, 611.
10. Jonathan Edwards, *A Treatise Concerning Religious Affections*, ed. John E. Smith (New Haven: Yale University Press, 1959). Subsequent references to this work will be incorporated within the text.
11. Paul Tillich, "The Word of God," in *Language: An Enquiry into Its Meaning and Function* (New York: Harper & Brothers, 1957), p. 133.
12. John A. Hutchinson, *Language and Faith: Studies in Sign, Symbol, and Meaning* (Philadelphia: The Westminster Press, 1963), p. 92.
13. Clyde A. Holbrook, "Jonathan Edwards and His Detractors," *Theology Today*, X (October 1953), 386.
14. Ola Elizabeth Winslow, *Jonathan Edwards, 1703-1758* (New York: The Macmillan Company, 1940), p. 145.
15. Alan Heimert, *Religion and the American Mind: From the Great Awakening to the Revolution* (Cambridge, Mass.: Harvard University Press, 1966), p. 116.
16. *Ibid.*
17. Perry Miller, *The New England Mind: The Seventeenth Century* (Cambridge, Mass.: Harvard University Press, 1954), p. 5.
18. James Carse, *Jonathan Edwards and the Visibility of God* (New York: Charles Scribner's Sons, 1967), p. 12; Charles Feidelson, Jr., *Symbolism and American Literature* (Chicago: University of Chicago Press, 1953), p. 101; Paul Elmer More, "Jonathan Edwards," in *A New England Group and Others: Shelburne Essays, Eleventh Series* (London: Constable & Co., n.d.), p. 42.
19. The Puritans cited five main counts against the style of seventeenth-century Anglican preaching: (1) its partiality for "strange and unexpected figures"; (2) its "wit"; (3) its passion for Latin and Greek quotations; (4) the "exaggerated importance" given to particular words or expressions; (5) its "illogical and unnecessary divisions and subdivisions." See W. Fraser Mitchell,

English Pulpit Oratory from Andrewes to Tillotson: A Study of Its Literary Aspects (London: Society for Promoting Christian Knowledge, 1932), p. 352.
The objections boiled down to the indictment of Bishop Croft of Hereford in 1675: " . . . they divide and subdivide into generals and particulars. . . ; then they study how to hook in this or that quaint sentence of Philosopher or Father, this or that nice speculation, endeavoring to couch all this in the most elegant language; in short, their main end is to show their Wit" (quoted in Mitchell, p. 363). Another treatment of these matters can be found in William Samuel Howell, *Logic and Rhetoric in England 1500-1700* (Princeton: Princeton University Press, 1956).

20. Quoted in Mitchell, pp. 364-365.

21. Ramus' manifesto appeared as the Preface to Omer Talon (Ramus' colleague), *Rhetorica* (1567). Ramus' ideas were made popular largely through Thomas Blount, *The Academie of Eloquence Containing a Compleat English Rhetoric* (1654), a work still widely read at Harvard and Yale during Edwards' day. For a full treatment of Ramist theory and the "plain style," see Perry Miller, *New England Mind: The Seventeenth Century*, ch. 12. The quotations cited in the text are from Miller, p. 321.

22. John Locke, *An Essay Concerning Human Understanding*, 2 vols. (London: G. Offor, *et al.*, 1819), Book III, ch. ii, section 1. Subsequent references to this work will be incorporated within the text.

23. Edwards, in *The Philosophy. . .*, ed. Townsend, p. 113.

24. *Ibid.*, p. 115.

25. *Ibid.*

26. *Ibid.*, p. 119.

27. *Ibid.*

28. *Ibid.*

29. Miller, *Errand*, p. 179.

30. Edwards, in *The Philosophy. . .*, ed. Townsend, p. 118.

31. *Ibid.*

32. "Indeed a person cannot have spiritual light without the word. But that does not argue, that the word properly causes that light. The mind cannot see the excellency of any doctrine, unless that doctrine be first in the mind. . . . So that the notions that are the subject matter of this light, are conveyed to the mind by the word of God; but that due sense of the heart, wherein this light formally consists, is immediately by the Spirit of God" ("The Divine and Supernatural Light," II,15).

33. Miller, *Errand*, p. 182.

34. Søren Kierkegaard, *Concluding Unscientific Postscript*, trans. David F. Swenson (Princeton: Princeton University Press, 1941), pp. 347-348. Italics mine.

35. R. F. Gill, "Theology and Literary Criticism," *Theology*, LXXIV (October 1971), 460.

36. Miller, *Errand,* p. 183.

37. Heimert, p. 116.

38. In "The True Excellency of a Gospel Minister" (II,957), Edwards described the minister as a "burning light," a person whose heart is filled with "the holy ardour of a spirit of true piety."

39. Richard Kroner, *Speculation and Revelation in the Age of Christian Philosophy* (Philadelphia: The Westminster Press, 1959), p. 107.

40. " . . . the systematic character of Augustine's and Kierkegaard's thought—and perhaps Luther's—seems almost *accidental*, compared with their urgency to communicate the glory they have seen"—Mary McDermott Shideler, "Art and the Art of Theology," *Theology Today*, XXVIII (July 1971), 147 (italics mine).

41. Jonathan Edwards, *Original Sin*, ed. Clyde A. Holbrook (New Haven: Yale University Press, 1970), p. 242.

42. *Ibid.*, p. 243.

43. Heimert, p. 116. Perry Miller refers to Samuel Willard, who approximately a hundred years before Witherspoon, said much the same thing about the importance of pulpit eloquence: through the power of words not only does our understanding need illumination, but much more do our wills and affections "need to be roused, quickened and drawn to their work" (Miller, *New England Mind: The Seventeenth Century*, p. 301).

44. Justus George Lawler, *The Christian Image: Studies in Religious Art and Poetry* (Pittsburgh: Duquesne University Press, 1966), pp. 86ff.

45. Gerardus van der Leeuw, *Sacred and Profane Beauty: The Holy in Art*, trans. David E. Green (New York: Holt, Rinehart and Winston, 1963), p. 306.

46. M. P. Ramsey, *Calvin and Art* (Edinburgh: The Moray Press, 1938), p. 23.

47. *Ibid.*, p. 15.

48. In Calvin, passages of vivid imagery such as the following are not uncommon: "Unless perchance it be unknown to us in whose power it lies to sustain this infinite mass of heaven and earth by his Word: by his nod alone sometimes to shake heaven with thunderbolts, to burn everything with lightnings, to kindle the air with flashes; sometimes to disturb it with various sorts of storms, and then at his pleasure to clear them away in a moment; to compel the sea, which by its height seems to threaten the earth with continual destruction, to hang as if in mid-air; sometimes to arouse it in a dreadful way with the tumultuous force of winds; sometimes, with waves quieted, to make it calm again!"—*Institutes of the Christian Religion*, ed. John T. McNeill, in The Library of Christian Classics (London: SCM Press, Ltd., 1960), I,v,6.

49. Herbert Read, *Icon and Idea: The Function of Art in the Development of Human Consciousness* (London: Faber and Faber, Ltd., 1955), p. 59.

50. Calvin, *Institutes*, II,ii,13.

51. Van der Leeuw, p. 266.

52. Paul Tillich, *Dynamics of Faith* (New York: Harper & Brothers, 1958), ch. 3.

53. Miller, *New England Mind: The Seventeenth Century*, p. 232.

54. *Ibid.*, p. 362.

55. See Miller's study of the New England jeremiad in *The New England Mind: From Colony to Province* (Cambridge, Mass.: Harvard University Press, 1953), pp. 29ff. Elsewhere Miller claims that by 1730 the type of sermon designed for "communal response," *i.e.*, the "revival" sermon, "was an almost perfected literary form, waiting only for someone [Edwards] to take it in hand" (*Jonathan Edwards*, p. 135). Despite ambivalence, Miller bends his interpretation of the sermon more towards art than religious proclamation.

56. Carse, p. 124.

57. Calvin, *Institutes*, II,ii,20; Edwards, *Religious Affections*, pp. 280-281.

Chapter 5

1. Perry Miller, ed., in Jonathan Edwards, *Images and Shadows of Divine Things* (New Haven: Yale University Press, 1948), p. 21.

2. John E. Smith, ed., in Edwards, *Religious Affections* (New Haven: Yale University Press, 1959), p. 8.

3. *Ibid.,* p. 9.

4. Paul R. Baumgartner, "Jonathan Edwards: The Theory Behind His Use of Figurative Language," *PMLA*, LXXVIII (September 1963), 324.

5. Alexander V. G. Allen, *Jonathan Edwards* (Boston: Houghton, Mifflin and Company, 1889), p. 104.

6. Joseph Haroutunian, *Piety Versus Moralism: The Passing of the New England Theology* (New York: Henry Holt and Company, 1932), p. 113.

7. Perry Miller, *Jonathan Edwards* (Cleveland: World Publishing Company, 1959), pp. 158, 160.

8. Ola Elizabeth Winslow, *Jonathan Edwards, 1703-1758* (New York: The Macmillan Company, 1940), p. 144.

9. See below, p. 139.

10. Winslow, p. 134.

11. Jonathan Edwards, *Original Sin,* ed. Clyde A. Holbrook (New Haven: Yale University Press, 1970), p. 124.

12. See Calvin, *Institutes,* II,i,5, for an account of the Reformed interpretation, plus a brief discussion of the Pelagian view of sin.

13. Jonathan Edwards, *Freedom of the Will,* ed. Paul Ramsey (New Haven: Yale University Press, 1957), p. 137.

14. *Ibid.,* p. 141.

15. Clarence H. Faust, in *Jonathan Edwards: Representative Selections,* eds. Faust and Thomas H. Johnson (New York: Hill and Wang, 1962), p. lxv.

16. Jonathan Edwards, *The Nature of True Virtue,* with Foreword by William K. Frankena (Ann Arbor: University of Michigan Press, 1960), ch. 4.

17. Douglas J. Elwood, *The Philosophical Theology of Jonathan Edwards* (New York: Columbia University Press, 1960), p. 64.

18. *Ibid.*

19. Joseph Haroutunian, "Jonathan Edwards: Theologian of the Great Commandment," *Theology Today,* I (April 1944), 370.

20. Calvin, *Institutes,* II,ii,15. A lucid explication of Calvin's defense of secular learning (*Institutes,* II,ii,13-17) is found in the Epilogue ("An Essay on Calvin's Defense of Secular Studies: His Doctrine of Common Grace") of Quirinus Breen's *John Calvin: A Study in French Humanism,* 2nd ed. (Archon Books, 1968), pp. 165-179.

21. Calvin, *Institutes,* I,iii,1.

22. Richard Kroner, *Speculation and Revelation in the Age of Christian Philosophy* (Philadelphia: Westminster Press, 1959), pp. 194ff. The same idea finds its modern expression in Barthian theology. "Faith," says Barth, "can never be lived except in a Notwithstanding: notwithstanding all that man finds himself and his fellow-men to be, notwithstanding all that he and his fellow-men may try to do"—*Church Dogmatics,* IV, I, eds. G. W. Bromiley and T. F. Torrance (Edinburgh: T. & T. Clark, 1956), p. 635.

23. Calvin, *Institutes,* I,i,1.

24. Rudolf Otto, *The Idea of the Holy,* 2nd ed., trans. John W. Harvey (London: Oxford University Press, 1950), p. 15.

25. "The real question is what man is in the presence of God, whether he can

stand before God; and such a question can only be answered by God Himself. 'The Holy Spirit assures us in Holy Scripture that our understanding is so smitten with blindness, our heart in its notions so evil and corrupt, in fact our whole nature so depraved, that we can do nothing else but sin until He Himself creates in us a new will' "—Wilhelm Niesel, *The Theology of Calvin,* trans. Harold Knight (London: Lutterworth Press, 1956), p. 80. The quotation is from Calvin.

26. "Hell, in whatever 'physical metaphors' it is depicted, for Calvin is essentially this: *'alienari ab omni Dei societate' —Institutes,* III,xxv,12 (p. 1008n in LCC, vol. 2). The editor compares Calvin's view with that of Milton in *Paradise Lost,* V, 877, specifically, Abdiel's address to Satan: "O alienate from God, O spirit accurst." The Reformers' view of natural man's self-sufficiency is treated in Wilhelm Pauck, *The Heritage of the Reformation* (Boston: Beacon Press, 1950), p. 9.

27. Paul Tillich, *The Protestant Era,* abridged edition, trans. James Luther Adams (Chicago: University of Chicago Press, 1957), p. xvi.

28. Sermons having this aim include "Unbelievers Contemn the Glory and Excellency of Christ"; "True Grace Distinguished from the Experience of Devils"; "Men Naturally Are God's Enemies"; "Natural Men in a Dreadful Condition"; "The Warnings of Scripture Are in the Best Manner Adapted to the Awakening and Conversion of Sinners."

29. Calvin, *Institutes,* III,iv,33.

30. James Carse, *Jonathan Edwards and the Visibility of God* (New York: Charles Scribner's Sons, 1967), p. 162.

31. Jonathan Edwards, "Directions for Judging of Persons' Experiences," in *Selections from the Unpublished Writings of Jonathan Edwards of America,* ed. Alexander B. Grosart (printed for private circulation, 1865), p. 184.

32. Calvin, *Institutes,* III,xxv,12 (italics mine).

33. *Ibid.*

34. His most effective sermons about damnation are: "The Eternity of Hell Torments"; "When the Wicked Shall Have Filled Up the Measure of Their Sin"; "The End of the Wicked Contemplated by the Righteous"; "The Future Punishment of the Wicked Unavoidable and Intolerable"; "The Justice of God in the Damnation of Sinners"; "Wrath Upon the Wicked to the Uttermost"; "Sinners in the Hands of an Angry God."

35. Paul Elmer More, *A New England Group and Others:* Shelburne Essays, Eleventh Series (London: Constable & Co., n.d.), p. 44.

36. Quoted by More, *ibid.*

37. Quoted by More, *ibid.*

38. This is not the case with the artists, according to F. O. Matthiessen: " . . . it is not accidental that our own modern writers, with their sense of what has been implied for our society by Edwards' excessive conscience and by our own moral preoccupation of Hawthorne and [Henry] James, should, whether impelled by O'Neill's feeling of chaotic disintegration or by Eliot's belief in the need for regeneration, still create characters whose inner torment makes them imagine that they are followed by the furies"—*American Renaissance* (New York: Oxford University Press, 1941), p. 339.

39. Winslow, ch. 11 ("Trouble in the Parish").

40. Oliver Wendell Holmes, *Pages from an Old Volume of Life: A Collection of Essays 1857-1881* (Boston: Houghton, Mifflin and Company, 1892), p. 369.

41. Oliver Wendell Holmes, *Over the Teacups* (Boston: Houghton, Mifflin and Company, 1892), p. 40.
42. *Ibid.*, p. 254.
43. William James, *The Varieties of Religious Experience: A Study in Human Nature* (London: Longmans, Green, and Co., 1902), p. 330.
44. Clarence Darrow, "The Edwardses and the Jukeses," *American Mercury,* VI (October 1925), 153.
45. Vernon Louis Parrington, *Main Currents in American Thought,* I (New York: Harcourt Brace and Company, 1927), 159.
46. Søren Kierkegaard, *The Concept of Dread,* trans. Walter Lowrie (Princeton: Princeton University Press, 1944), p. 139.
47. Miller, *Jonathan Edwards,* p. 137.
48. Richard Hofstadter, *Anti-Intellectualism in American Life* (New York: Alfred A. Knopf, 1963).
49. Winslow, p. 137.
50. Elwood, p. 2.
51. Thomas H. Johnson, in Jonathan Edwards, *Representative Selections,* eds. Faust and Johnson, p. cxi.
52. Jonathan Edwards, *Observations Upon Particular Passages of Scriptures,* in *The Works of President Edwards,* 4 vols. (New York: Robert Carter and Brothers, 1869), III, 548.
53. Peter Gay, *A Loss of Mastery: Puritan Historians in Colonial America* (Berkeley and Los Angeles: University of California Press, 1966), p. 108.
54. For an intelligent and far-ranging assessment of Edwards' detractors, see Clyde A. Holbrook, "Jonathan Edwards and His Detractors," *Theology Today,* X (October 1953), 384-396.
55. Quoted in Otto, p. 99.
56. Nicolas Berdyaev, *The Destiny of Man* (New York: Harper & Row, 1960), p. 179.
57. Miller, *Jonathan Edwards,* p. 147.
58. H. Richard Niebuhr, in *Christian Ethics: Sources of the Living Tradition,* eds. Niebuhr and Waldo Beach (New York: Ronald Press, 1955), p. 380.
59. Carse, p. 161.
60. Søren Kierkegaard, *The Sickness Unto Death,* in *Fear and Trembling/The Sickness . . .* (New York: Doubleday & Co., 1954), p. 214.

Chapter 6

1. William E. Rowley, "The Puritan's Tragic Vision," *The New England Quarterly,* XVII (September 1944), 417.
2. Robert Spiller, *The Cycle of American Literature: An Essay in Historical Criticism* (New York: The Free Press, 1967), p. 11.
3. Alan Heimert, *Religion and the American Mind: From the Great Awakening to the Revolution* (Cambridge, Mass.: Harvard University Press, 1966), p. 64; Douglas J. Elwood, *The Philosophical Theology of Jonathan Edwards* (New York: Columbia University Press, 1960), p. 87.
4. Perry Miller, *The New England Mind: The Seventeenth Century* (Cambridge, Mass.: Harvard University Press, 1954), p. 38.
5. *Ibid.*, p. 26.
6. John Calvin, *Institutes of the Christian Religion,* ed. John T. McNeill, in Library of Christian Classics (London: SCM Press, Ltd., 1960), III,xxi,1.

7. Jonathan Edwards, *Treatise on Grace*, in *Selections from the Unpublished Writings of Jonathan Edwards of America*, ed. Alexander B. Grosart (printed for private circulation, 1865), p. 19.

8. Ola Elizabeth Winslow, *Jonathan Edwards, 1703-1758* (New York: The Macmillan Company, 1940), p. 309.

9. Grosart, ed., *Treatise on Grace*, in *Selections*, p. 11.

10. Edwards, *Treatise on Grace*, pp. 22-25.

11. *Ibid.*, p. 32.

12. *Ibid.*, p. 33.

13. *Ibid.*, pp. 36-45.

14. *Ibid.*, p. 55.

15. Alexander V. G. Allen, *Jonathan Edwards* (Boston: Houghton, Mifflin and Company, 1889), p. 313.

16. Jonathan Edwards, *The Nature of True Virtue*, with Foreword by William K. Frankena (Ann Arbor: University of Michigan Press, 1960), p. 19.

17. *Ibid.*, p. 20.

18. *Ibid.*, pp. 22-23.

19. Ibid., p. 9.

20. H. Richard Niebuhr, *Christian Ethics: Sources of the Living Tradition*, eds. Niebuhr and Waldo Beach (New York: The Ronald Press, 1955), p. 389.

21. *Ibid.*

22. Winslow, ch. 2.

23. Perry Miller, ed., in Edwards, *Images or Shadows of Divine Things* (New Haven: Yale University Press, 1948), p. 4.

24. Joseph Haroutunian, ed., in Calvin, *Commentaries*, in Library of Christian Classics (London: SCM Press, Ltd., 1958), pp. 41-43.

25. Peter Gay, *A Loss of Mastery: Puritan Historians in Colonial America* (Berkeley and Los Angeles: University of California Press, 1966), p. 104.

26. Richard Kroner, *The Religious Function of Imagination* (New Haven: Yale University Press, 1941), pp. 46-47.

27. See C. C. Goen, "Jonathan Edwards: A New Departure in Eschatology," *Church History*, XXVIII (March 1959), 25-40, for an analysis of what Goen calls "the content, novelty and source" of Edwards' millennial ideas. Of interest also is Edwards' "Notes on the Apocalypse," an unpublished notebook of 208 numbered pages started in 1723 and written over a period of some thirty-five years. Unnoticed by Goen, Heimert, and Miller, the notebook reveals Edwards' lifelong preoccupation with eschatology. See Stephen J. Stein, "A Notebook on the Apocalypse by Jonathan Edwards," *The William and Mary Quarterly*, XXIV (October 1972), 623-634.

28. Peter Toon, *Puritans, the Millennium and the Future of Israel: Puritan Eschatology 1600-1660*, ed. Toon (London: James Clarke & Co., 1970), p. 25.

29. *Ibid.*, p. 26.

30. *Ibid.*

31. Quoted in Heimert, p. 52.

32. Heimert, p. 130.

33. Perry Miller, *Jonathan Edwards* (Cleveland: World Publishing Company, 1959), p. 198.

34. Heimert, pp. 125-126.

35. Goen, 36.

36. Perry Miller, *Errand Into the Wilderness* (New York: Harper & Row, 1964), p. 238.

37. Miller, *Jonathan Edwards*, p. 285.
38. Edwards, *The Nature of True Virtue*, p. 23.
39. Elwood, pp. 6-9.
40. Joseph Haroutunian, "Jonathan Edwards: Theologian of the Great Commandment," *Theology Today*, I (April 1944), 361-362.

Index of Names

171

Index of Edwards' Works